AGENDA

WELSH ISSUE

AGENDA

CONTENTS

POEMS

TWO CHOSEN YOUNG BROADSHEET POETS

NOTES FOR BROADSHEET POETS:

BIOGRAPHIES

Front cover: ***Codiad Haul (Sunrise)***, 109 x 69cm, mixed media, 2007
by **Mary Lloyd Jones** who was born in Devil's Bridge in 1934. She
trained at Cardiff College of Art and has exhibited widely at home
and abroad, including solo shows in New York, London, Cologne
and Oslo, and recent shows in France and Italy.

Inspired by the Welsh landscape and, in particular, the man-
made marks on that landscape, her bold expressionist paintings
are noted for their use of vibrant and rich colour.

She was recently awarded an Honorary Doctorate by the
University of Wales.

This painting, along with other works of hers, is in the Martin
Tinney Gallery, 18 St. Andrew's Crescent, Cardiff CF10 3DD
Tel: 029 2064 1411, www.artwales.com

It is printed here by kind permission of the Martin Tinney
Gallery.

Editorial

Very many thanks to all the contributors who demonstrate the creative and enormous spirit of Welsh poetry both in English and in Welsh, and to all the readers whose appreciation is as necessary to the journal as its writers.

Many thanks also to the Welsh Books Council for its generous support.

Special mention must go to **Patrick McGuinness**, poet, Welshman and Professor at St. Anne's College, Oxford, for his advice, help and support.

Contributors include full-blooded Welsh poets in both Welsh and English, those resident and/or teaching in Wales and those with a genuine closeness to Wales.

I hope you all enjoy this special issue which has grown larger than originally planned, but how could *Agenda* turn down such a wealth of talent, such music in words, such exciting work. It has been a pleasure working with such heart-warming and encouraging Welsh people on this issue.

Further issues of *Agenda* during this year will be **a double 50th Anniversary issue**, and **a special single issue on C.H. Sisson**, guest-edited by Charlie Louth, the grandson of C.H. Sisson.

Visit **the website** www.agendapoetry.co.uk for poetry supplements and paintings, for Broadsheets for young poets and artists, and much more.

In tandem with this issue: an online Welsh supplement of poems and paintings. Also, an introduction to Lynette Roberts, Welsh poetess (*Collected Poems*, Carcanet) by Patrick McGuinness (whose recent pamphlet is reviewed here, in the Omnium Gatherum of Welsh Books by W.S. Milne); and an essay by Ian Gregson, 'The New Women's Poetry in Wales'.

Of special note: a new edition of *The Canterbury Tales: A Selection* has recently come out from Penguin Classics, chosen, translated and edited by the Welsh trustee of *Agenda*, ColinWilcockson. Chaucer's original fourteenth century Middle English is paralleled with Wilcockson's refreshingly readable, fluent modern prose, and illuminates the latter's scholarly insights into the language and themes of Chaucer's *General Prologue* and his best-loved tales.

Please do not forget to **re-new your subscriptions** and to encourage your friends to subscribe! A cut-out subscription form is at the back of his issue.

Patricia McCarthy.

For David Jones' enthusiasts –
a limited number of back issues of *Agenda* Editions are still available:
David Jones: *Letters to William Hayward*, edited by Colin Wilcockson
David Jones: *The Roman Quarry and other sequences*, edited by
                    Harman Grisewood and René Hague
David Jones: *The Kensington Mass*
David Jones: *Ten Letters*
For prices and availability email the *Agenda* office: editor@agendapoetry.co.uk or phone: 01435 873703 or write to: The Wheelwrights, Fletching Street, Mayfield, East Sussex TN20 6TL.

Introduction

Welcome to this Welsh issue, a first ever for *Agenda* in all its fifty years, which carries in its breath a great amount of *hwyl*.

Agenda has always had a special connection with David Jones. The lettering AGENDA and CONTENTS was specially done by David Jones for *Agenda* many years ago, and remains its consistent logo. The bard's name, Aneirin, is given to one of David Jones's personae, Aneirin Merddyn Lewis, who carries out the bard's orders: 'It is our duty to sing' – as do all the poets in this special issue. In John Matthew's book, *Taliesin* (The Aquarian Press, 1991), Matthews discusses the ancient origin of the old Irish word, *uath*, meaning 'poetic art'. The synonym for this, *awen*, in Welsh is linked with *seis*, musical art, *cluas*, hearing, and *anal*, breath. 'The poet breathes in the *awan*, hears it and gives forth in musical speech or song.'

All the poets herein justly earn the title 'Carpenters of Song'. David Jones referred to this very title: 'The bards of an earlier Wales referred to themselves as "carpenters of song"/ Carpentry suggests a fitting together, and … the English word "artist" means, at root, someone concerned with a fitting of some sort'.

In an enlightening, scholarly book on David Jones by Paul Robichaud who has a poem in this issue, fairly recently published, *Making the Past Present: David Jones, the Middle Ages and Modernism* (The Catholic University of America Press, Washington D.C., 2007), I read that Sir Ifor Williams noted the same thing: 'the bards of an earlier Wales referred to themselves as "*carpenters of song*"'.

Dylan Thomas, a mentor of my earlier years, extends this 'carpentry' image. In a letter to Henry Treece, 18th May 1938, he also talks about his poems being '*hewn*'. He refers to poems as 'watertight compartments'. 'Much of the obscurity is due to rigorous compression; the last thing they do is to flow; they are much rather hewn.'

David Jones would probably not agree, however, with poems being 'watertight compartments' i.e. stopping the flow. He had an illuminating experience thirty five years before publishing *The Anathemata* in 1952. He was staying at Capel y Ffin when the water in the house suddenly stopped flowing. He and his friend, René Hague (who edited *Agenda* Editions' *The Roman Quarry and other sequences* by David Jones – see Editorial page for availability), set off on foot and found the source of the stream that had been deliberately blocked. They triumphantly freed the waters.

As Michael Symmons Roberts says, in his interesting essay 'Freeing the Waters – Poetry in a Parched Culture' in *Necessary Steps*, a collection of essays on poetry, elegy, walking and spirit, edited by David Kennedy (Shearsman, 2007): 'This image of "freeing the waters" continued to resonate with Jones.' Symmons Roberts suggests that this image of Jones freeing the waters is as resonant now, half a century later. He declares optimistically for poetry, 'However parched our culture might become, there is still water in abundance. The stream has been diverted – perhaps wilfully – but it has not dried up.' Far from it, as witnessed here.

Gerard Manley Hopkins was entranced by the image of St.Winefred's Well, to which he often walked from St. Beuno, where miraculous cures were meant to take place. He felt the Well had healed him spiritually. Although the fresh, clean water was contained there, its spring filled Hopkins 'with devotion', particularly its lavish flow of *aglaon hudor* (bright water). This idea of containment, of binding yet freeing (also evident in Hopkins' 'Penmaen Pool'), was very much what David Jones went along with. According to Michael Symmons Roberts, Waldo Williams, the Welsh poet, felt similarly. He described his religion and his native language – which he believed to be inextricably linked – as 'a large room with narrow walls'. i.e. a binding to make free.

Hopkins himself, though obviously not Welsh, did think of Wales as his spiritual home and even took lessons in the Welsh language. At one point, he tried to translate *Cinderella* from English into Welsh. We are told this in a very readable, very recently published biography, *Gerard Manley Hopkins: A Life* (Viking Press) by Paul Mariani. He recalls how Hopkins loved the Welsh language – "'all vowels", which "run off the tongue like oil by diphthongs and by triphthongs" – as much as he loved the Welsh landscape', particularly that around St. Beuno. Mariani also quotes Hopkins' translation into Welsh of the beginning of a latin poem attributed to St. Francis Xavier, and his intention to buy, with money from winning a round of the 'spelling bee' with the monks, the 'Complete Works of Goronwy Owen "or some other great Welsh poet"'. This biography is replete with interesting little known details. If it has a fault, it is that, in my view, there is too much paraphrasing of Hopkins' poems. This makes Hopkins very accessible for those not too familiar with his work, but can be aggravating for those who know his poems intimately and can roll them off their own tongues.

My own personal experience of Wales was in journeying backwards and forwards as a child and young adult between Ireland and England. The long, slow Holyhead boat train in those days was full of drunks, emergency communication cords, uniformed guards, a mantra of names that slid past like Colwyn Bay, Prestatyn, Rhyl, Llandudno, wonderful reddish rocks carved into sculptures by the sea, golden sands and white rows of caravans even then. On good days only, we lived with the Welsh mountains that appeared from the Irish coastline like visions over the sea. The singsong sound of the Welsh language gabbled by porters on stations where the train always stopped sounded different from the Irish Gaelic I had learnt for five or six years in Ireland. I remember memorising by heart the longest train-station name in the world, never mind on Anglesey island: *Llanfairpwllgwyngyllgogerychwyrndrobwillantysiliogogogoch* and racing my sisters to see who could get to the end of it in one breath. Pronouncing it was a poetic patter in itself.

Time, now, to open the pages and listen to the 'carpenters of song'. David Jones, who saw all the arts as one, said (see Tim Smith-Laing's essay in this issue):

'Poetry, painting, carving are only as different as oil paint and watercolour'.

David Jones seemed to think, however, that, even in his day, the poet was lamentably removed from being 'the custodian, rememberer, embodier and voice of the people'. Back, then, to the following pages whose poets surely refute this statement in proving themselves inheritors of the ancient bards: true 'carpenters of song'.

A line surfaces from Dylan Thomas: 'And I sang in my chains like the sea'.

Patricia McCarthy

Menna Elfyn

Cerdd Gocos

Hi oedd y wraig wrth ein drws,
hwyr brynhawn, basged mewn llaw,
lliain gwyn yn orchudd
fel Cymun heb ei godi.
Yna'n sydyn, clegar o gocos,
islais o 'fara lawr'
ar bapur di-saim,
a'r fargen ar y ford.

Adeg swpera wedyn,
byddai mam yn arllwys
tosturi at y wreigan,
ar daith o Benclawdd i Gwm Tawe,
mewn bws decer dwbwl.
A theimlo'r rhyddhad
i'w siwrne tua thre
fod yn ysgafnach:
sylltau yn lle cregyn
– wrth i'n ffyrc anturio'n ffyrnig.

Mae ei gwên gyda mi o hyd,
yn toddi un â chroeso fy mam;
dwy siâp calon fel cocos,
y rhai fu'n adeiladu
eu tai ar dywod
cyn i'r llanw daenu
ei gotwm ei hun o ewyn.

A'r wraig gocos?
Tonnau gwallt olchwyd dan het,
a'i siôl yn rhidens ar draeth,
machlud ar ddŵr,
fel finegr da
sy'n brathu gwefus.

Awelon haf broGŵyr
yn chwythu ein mynd a'n dyfod—
gan ddadbacio ennyd o bicnic.
A'r llun rhyfeddol hwnnw
ohoni'n llenwi'r peint cwrw
drosodd a throsodd,
fel diniweidrwydd yn disgyn
yn y gwydr niwlog,

Gwag.

The Cocklewoman

The late afternoon caller,
her basket, a linen coverlet,
like the laying of communion;
then suddenly, the cackle
of cockles, and *'bara lawr'*,
a falling tone on greaseproof,
and the deal's deliverance.

Later, my mother at suppertime
would season pity on the poor
lady, for her long journey,
on a double-decker bus
from Gower to Pontardawe;
gladdened too at her return
all the lighter,
shillings instead of shells,
as we sifted our forks like adventurers.

Her smile is still alive,
melting into my mother's welcome;
two heartshaped cockles
who built their homes
on sand, before the tide's curl,

and a shawl's fringe on the shore;
sunset on water, and skin
a fine malt vinegar,
burning lip.

And ah, the salt air of *Gŵyr*,
days of spins, unpacking,
our picnics, near sea lavender.

But one gaze still lingers,
her sacrament at our door,
the beer pint catches,
to me in the Manse,
it was the sound
of innocence descending,
a coming of age:
that emptying, emptying cry.

*bara lawr: laverbread
*Gŵyr: Welsh word for Gower

Ôl-nodyn

Marwolaethau? Edliw wnant
y rhai byw, ei diffyg
sylw at agosatrwydd.

Cans yn y diwedd, ing
yw'r mawlgan a'r ddameg,
y modd yr aeth un wraig

frau, yn ei phwysau heibio:
addurnodau'n disgyn
yn y meddwl. Hyhi,

a gerddodd drwy'r cagle
i yrru ei geiriau, cario
hyd at yr edau, noethni brwydrau,

cyn clwydo un noson,
gwisg nos sidan, anfflamadwy,
parti i un, bri gwirodydd

a thabledi i ddiffodd einioes.
Dyma ddiweddglo
adroddwyd yn dda,

hicio nodion 'post it',
asio eiddo at ei etifedd
mor gyfewin ag anadl

gan adael 'run dedlein,
heb ei anfon. A neb gartre
i syllu ar gyrffiw

sy'n rhwystro'r ffordd. Heb her
yr haul chwaith. Gadael –
yn lân, heb atgof ar y lôn.

End note

i.m Martha Gellhorn

Obits are meant to reproach
the living; their lack of
attention to intimation.

In the end, death
is our paean, our parable.
How one frail woman

takes it in her stride,
grace notes descending
in the mind. She,

who'd walked through pismire
to wire her words; carried
her wears through wars

and retired one evening:
silky nightdress, non-flammable,
a party for one on spirits,

taking pills to nub life out.
This was a dying
well-delivered,

notching 'post it' notes-
matching piece to person
as exact as life can ever be,

leaving no deadline
hanging. And nobody home
to notice the curfew

on paths or the dare of sunlight.
Leaving not even a memory
on any lane.

(*translated by* the author)

Mererid Hopwood

Ym Mhenrhyn Gŵyr

Ym Mhenrhyn Gŵyr
does neb a ŵyr,
pan fo'r hwyr yn casglu'r golau,
sut un yw'r gŵr
sy'n dwyn y dŵr,
does neb yn siŵr – 'mond amau;

pwy piau'r côl
sy'n denu'n ôl
yr ewyn gwyn o'r traethau,
a'i fagu'n dynn
yn ei freichiau gwyn,
tra bo'r bae yn wylo am ddagrau;

pwy 'ddwed y drefn
nes, wysg eu cefn,
mae'n hawlio'r tonnau'n ofer –
'rôl hanner oes
o dynnu'n groes
cânt lifo'n ôl bob amser;

a hithau'n drai
a'r môr yn llai
mae rhywrai'n eto'n gwybod,
er bod hi'n hwyr
ym Mhenrhyn Gŵyr
daw'r llanw'n llwyr ryw ddiwrnod.

Down on the Gower

Down on the Gower
nobody knows,
as the dark sucks in the light,
who might it be
that steals the sea;
no one can know tonight.

Whose is the lap
that draws them back,
the wavelets from the beaches,
whose arms fold them,
hug them, hold them,
as the bay weeps for salty tears?

Whose law is this
that calls them out,
those waves he holds so vainly?
After half a life
of stress and strife
they will return, and surely

the wise still know
that even though
the sea tonight is smaller,
there will come a day
when the waves reach the bay
and the tide returns to the Gower.

Translated by **David Eurig-Davies**

Note:

Some night before Christmas I happened to be on the beach watching the ebbing waves. For the first time ever, I realised that the water did not want to leave the shore at all. If the waves wanted to go they would face the other way. Against their will they go because something is pulling them away. Of course, this pulling is in vain because, every time, they come back. And it's something like that for all of us I expect ... It's difficult to believe that I have lived for forty+ years without realising this basic truth, but that, simply is the background to this poem. The Gower Peninsula was the first area of outstanding beauty designated in Britain.

Darnau Tawelwch

Y darn du rhwng
yr ennyd a'r funud fach
sy'n aros oes yn hirach,

y darn llwyd rhwng
diwedd y môr a'r gorwel,

y darn gwyn rhwng
gair a gair yn gorwedd,

y darn arian rhwng
dau enaid a dwy anal,

y darn aur rhwng
dwy wên a'r ddwy yn dyner,

cyfri'r rhain yw cyfrinach tawelwch –
y darnau sydd â'u lliwiau'n
deimlad anniffiniadwy
yn bod o'm mewn – dim byd mwy.

Fragments of Silence

The fragment of black between
the instant and the fleeting minute
that lasts an aeon longer,

The fragment of grey between
the sea's end and the horizon,

The fragment of white between
one word and another lying,

The fragment of silver between
two souls, two breaths,

The fragment of gold between
two smiles, both so tender,

Counting these is the secret of silence,
the fragments with their colours
an indefinable feeling
within me –
nothing more.

Translated by **David Eurig-Davies**

Bro

Un haf, amser maith yn ôl,
i wlad yr alaw hudol,
i nyth y gân, daeth y gog
i waeddu'i hawl gelwyddog,
ac i roi ei geiriau hi
yn enwau dierth inni.
Crio'i hawl mewn synnau cras
un diwrnod – dwyn y deyrnas.

Yn y fro, ni fu yr un
nodau yn canu wedyn,
ac ar goll aeth geiriau'r gân
a'n henwau hen ein hunan,

Nawr y gog piau'n bro i gyd,
a'n haf a'n gaeaf hefyd …

Ers i'r haf a'i arafwch
droi yr allt a'r perci'n drwch
â dail gwyllt, 'ond ôl y gân
ac adlais sy'n y goedlan,
ôl rhyw air sy'n alaw'r rhos,
darn o air draw yn aros.

Dyna i gyd, a heno gwn
mai mud o hyd fydd y gair hwn.

Home Patch

One Summer, long long ago,
to the country of seductive song,
to its very heart, came a cuckoo,
to croak its lying claim,
and force its words,
a stranger's words on us.

Shouting full a foreign call
and one day – stealing all.

In this land no note,
no song was heard thereafter.
Even the words that sang
our very names
in this land were lost.

Now the cuckoo owns the grove,
in Summer, in Winter too.

Since the slow Summer
filled the copse and fields
with its rich leaves,
only a trace of a song,
an echo in the forest,
a part of a word in the music of the moor,
holds on.

That's all, and I know
that now,
this word is mute.

Translated by **David Eurig-Davies**

Andrew McNeillie

Literalist

The thrush deceives no one.
The curlew betrays no one.
The lark inspires no one.
Ravens never say never.
Nor does the yellow-hammer
sing about bread or cheese
in the beggared hedgerow.

The stormcock's no herald.
The terrace peacock isn't proud.
The nightingale never ravishes.
Swallows in number
don't make a summer
nor the wild-goose skein
bring autumn again.

The Shadow of a Blackbird

It wasn't snowing and it wasn't going to snow.
Snow had become a thing I used to know,
a metaphor whited out of every latitude I knew.
So when I mentioned it, I thought of you.

So winter might have looked to its laurels,
no longer variegated, no longer what it was.
And the blackbird stranded in its branches
looked the shadow of a blackbird too.

The Wild Thorne

The day stands on formality,
timing its entry, like a bride.

How could she be late?
What might that be beside?

What suspense of cloud.
What gauze, and hand to hair...

Byron Beynon

Brynmawr

for Claude Powis

When the sea dropped
clear away,
the past happened,
the iron jaws of a hardboiled place,
winter comes easily
to the high town of the country.

Waun Helygen – Marsh of the Willows,
caught at the head of the valley
the air rarefied,
a raw presence
as the snow covers
the old tracks on mountain ridges.
Moonlight and singeing frost,
remote cairns on Llangattock moors,
the wind cracks the wanderer in half.
Adrift Ebbw Fach?
History can dry you up
with only echoes of the forge,
the ice begins to weep,
slow on a big hill.

Cefn Sidan

Before the arrival of places and the breaking of silences
I knew these elusive dunes and sea,
a wonder of landscape soft-running
as my hour-glass of childhood met the laughing air;
a myriad grains each with a history,
razor shells, jellyfish, footprints,
all become one in that tunnelled memory
where time is a perpetual summer.
The gulls within their portrait of coastline
sense the familiar ebb and flow
as a magnet of sun
propels their day across sky and shore.
The cartography of then,
indisputable and true
the white foam surviving
with the burning salt in my hair.

Tinplate

This is the rain my father knew.
My mother would see him to the door

as he left for work
at the tinplate plant.

A worker for all seasons,
his continental shift

sounded like a dance,
a geological movement

over a quarter of a century;
mornings, afternoons, nights,

two of each as he'd wait
for the one weekend holiday per month,

the stop-fortnight of summer
as July closed and August began.

His coil of days,
the overtime for extra pay

inside a fork-lift truck.
I still see and hear him leave,

his uncomplaining silence
I search as the tinplate shifts.

Tony Curtis

Reaching Yr Achub

i.m. Peter Prendergast

This is what you would have wished:
when they heard, the quarry men offered a gift,
took your sons up with them
to the face above the town
to choose a slab of slate from the rare, green vein.

Dressed, polished and inscribed: *Painter and teacher*
it will weather through the hard winters
in this corner of Bethesda's cemetery. Rest easy,
Peter, on your right shoulder the Penrhyn quarry,
at your left Ynys Mon and then the Irish Sea.

Two at Manorbier

On the occasion of the wedding of Gareth and Madeleine

You are that seal's head bobbing between crests
as you lie on the waltzing board
feeling each swell, taking the sea's pulse
waiting for the next wave,
just one more, your last of the day,
to sweep you back to a point between
the castle and the white bell tower
to the sloping sand and smoothed pebbles

where she sits waiting:
and when you call through the waves' crash,
when you raise your arms,
she shields her eyes against the dropping sun
to pick you out, and smiles;
though you can't see, you know, she smiles.

The Blue Grave Of Corfu

Each morning in the half-light
the young Serbian boys slip over the side of the boat
into the water.
            It is Winter –
the straits are inky dark and cold.

They turn over and press their bony heads
into the five fathoms.
            They have been rowed
far enough from Vidos Island
so that the waters can bed them.
There's little left but their bones and,
skeletal, they dive out of history.

This is after the long march, tactically away
from the Austrians, past the sniping Albanians,
through the callous snows of the mountains.
They have left behind the old and the pregnant women:
in national dress some are hanged from crucifixes.

The army has stumbled on, leaving the fallen, the weak.
They have danced with dysentery,
            have laid down
with tuberculosis, typhus. Now they shrink back
into the loneliness of themselves, huddled
in the make-shift tents of British sails and oars.
From the gnarled olive and rocky island
the boat ferries back and forth to their common blue grave
and Charon's the Greek.

In the summer months of that year
the azure waters grow warm
            and for five more summers
after the war, the Corfiots will cast no nets there,
take no fish fed from the blue grave of the Serbs.

The sands will marrow their limbs
to an ivory white.
            They compose a brief coral reef;
there are lobsters and silver bass that were their flesh.

Chris Kinsey

End-of-year Chorus

for Glenda Beagan

Even the lightest feet churn
this rain-whipped earth.
The Severn swirls brown from
too much run-off. I think of how
you'd like to climb Twt Hill and watch the Clwyd.

Evening's black-brown birds
would be your delight:
two dippers barrel over the rapids,
blackbirds squabble for roosts
and a moorhen's wake

makes a Vee at a day where
the sun can't be bothered to set.
As wrens flit nets of dead goosegrass
and the tangle of brambles,
I sense you most, limed by love,

calming the agitations of a mind
flapping free of memory
as you struggle to help
in that panicky zone
between standing and sitting.

Your caring gives no vent
to a clamour like these birds –
all outrage and fierce cries.
Year-round,
your songs keep sweet notes.

Leaving Bardsey

for Maggie Hampton

Seals croon the turning tide
as we wait for the boat,
down at the Cafn.
Fog mottles and drifts –
dumbing all senses.

You ask, 'What noise
are the seals making?'
Most shy of singers, I moor
close to your ear's cove
to sing seal, make mer-moan.

'That's it,' you smile,
'I turned my hearing aid
right up and I heard them.'
Now the fog won't budge,
just the sea's wash

seeming to whisper:
Ynys Enlli,
Ynys Enlli,
Ynys Enlli.

Ian Gregson

Dolgarrog Flood, 1925

The church bells woke me, sounding wrong,
too close, too loud, and pealing too late
across the dream I'd caught of Flanders
from my father, muddy meadows,
broken oaks, the trenches awash,
mingled with Dolgarrog when water
smashed our cottage open – as others,
four years later, would be smashed,
when Wall Street crashed – for water,
and no human hand, had rung the bells
of the church, uprooting its nave,
lifting away its graves and altar,
forcing it all downhill
towards our cottage which its hands
turned inside out and emptied
into the cataract that floated
my mattress under the speeding night
towards the aluminium works
whose seven furnaces exploded
adding hell to the high water
where the vicar, fisher of men,
rescued me and sat me on the roof
from where I could see the future
and the past, a village upside down,
the no man's land a shocking force
out of the dark behind our backs
extended miles across the valley,
breaking the fields - the walls and streets
under water, shoes and hats,
a chalice, kettles and legs of chairs,
slowing and sinking as the surface fell.

The Stuffing Boxes

I love those words but often I can't grasp
their live load: *Harry saw the young*
Cuban smile in the binnacle light –
the novelist, who knows such names,
has sometimes thought inside their weft,
has skippered boats or broken wild horses.
Reading you detect distraught sinew,
muscle in despair you're sure
they must've felt, and access opened
where the gate is normally padlocked
at the bridge to the landscaped island.
So you're half on, half off that boat
where Harry puts one hand on the
water manifold, the cylinders
and then the stuffing boxes, and the cloud
reflected in the water keeps
receding so your boat can never
enter the patch where it sits.
And yet it's marvellous to embark
and also know I needn't stay
on board, and watch my train shift
the setting west of Abergele,
seeing the coast off Cienfuegos,
Harry tightening the grease cups
a turn and a half each.

Christine Evans

Hovers

Like the otter's secret havens,
daybeds deep in rushes where he rests
from boistering or waits for dark
and the whistle far-off from the holt,

hovers

are the breathing-spaces,
recoveries of saved calm:
hushed but quivering with energy
within earshot of the river

(coming round, coming back,
watching light move round a room,
not thinking how might mind and body mesh;
delighting in the creature self).

Just a long night's wait
And a day's sail away

My dreamed father tells me this
in a language that wakes me wondering
was it more like Welsh, or Latin,
and how its promise floods me, instantly.

Rising

though it is still solid dark
there's a sense of shift,
of light rousing, beginning
to stir and stretch beyond the mountains

and then, one breath of wind
that lifts the hair, an exhalation
alive with all that's visible
in that other world over the horizon

wakes, in a heartbeat, an image:
my husband's mother, ten years gone,
rising, reaching, on tiptoe, to brush away cobwebs
with the silver arc of a goose wing feather

Duncan Bush

Avedon's Drifters

Richard Avedon, 1923-2004

After wall on wall of
the important, fashionable or glamorous,
famed pictures of the famous
in his 2002 exhibition at the Met, it's unexpectedly

in the last gallery-space
that we confront
Richard Avedon's portraits
of sky-eyed losers –

these shrunken-bellied rueful old boys
dapper in Western-style duds,
or no-longer-youthful tumbleweeds
with a gleam of wildness not yet wholly dulled –

itinerants
encountered at obscure and remote
locations undepicted (each subject
framed on white stark as for an ID shot)

but commemorated in all the poetry
and desolation
of a road-number, a named place
passed through once:

'Clarence Lippard, drifter,
Interstate 80, Sparks, Nevada, 1983';

'James Kimberlin, drifter,
State Road 11, Hobbs, New Mexico, 1980';

'Clifford Feldner, unemployed ranch hand,
Golden, Colorado, 1983';

'Alan Silvey, drifter,
Route 93, Chloride, Nevada, 1980':

lives gone awry in America, though each
in Whitman's words
was a child once
sleeping in his mother's bedroom.

And we are moved
by these faces, by their grievous
dignity, we are halted
in passing (see how scrutinising faces

among a queue-dense wet-Sunday public are
ennobled by sympathy,
by a troubled intentness
– this on the faces of urbanite Noo Yawkers

who in the pavement's flow ignore daily
and all week the sight
of other persons
adrift, deracinate or feral).

Yet something too shrinks back
at these photographs,
some diffidence or
delicacy,

since which of us could imagine singling out
each out-of-luck stranger
in a bar forecourt or at a roadside,
brokering the fee for the shots?

Perhaps in all human empathy,
all art, a ruthless prurience lies visible
like a watermark
at a certain angle to the light.

Either way, here on display,
in that moment's monochrome daylight
not harsh but printed
freckle-clear, pore-clear

and bigger than life-size
are these vagabond drinkers
or feckless workhands
whom ordinarily the tactful eye slides past,

undependable or disappointment-wounded
sons or husbands
of the fugitive kind, caught
before they edge away out of focus again:

guys of whom all their lives it was said
that they were never, ever there.

Fragonard's Lovers

Sundays in The Frick:
Deep-piled, dim-lit, a quiet
Not mortuary but

Mausoleum-like.
Here Fragonard's lovers live
Their garden idyll

Overshadowed by
Irreal, blue trees whose crowns
Swell anvil-shaped like

Summer thunder-clouds…
Mme. Du Barry who once
Refused these paintings

(But never suave Louis)
is bones; and old Mr. Frick,
Whose excellence of

Taste in art was fed
By wealth derived from whisky,
Coke and steel, is too.

Yet these rococo
Darlings of Fragonard's still
Entrance and enchant –

They move us with their
Infant-like impatience for
Uncertain joys. We

See there is no time
Beyond these instants for this
Flush-cheeked belle, her swain;

The roses are all
But overblown, and Cupid's
Asleep, bored by what

He foreknows in love's
Triumphal crowning with that
Wreath of fresh-cut blooms.

Edward Storey

A Second Adam

There is a world between two worlds
the heart keeps secret. It still would not reject
the place that proves the certainties of love
or claim the other which it cannot own.
Such unexpected joy might then remain
without an habitation, unless it find
another world in which to safely breathe –
somewhere like Eden, where we could stand
stripped of convention and believe
there are no boundaries to flesh or bone.

It is a world where love can still express
longings of which the earth would not approve –
or, if it does, bruise them again with shame.
For who has not been tempted in his time
to say 'I will be Adam twice' and gazed
(not lustfully) on slender Eve?
Yet there is love that can transcend the eye
which does not need a fool's mask or decree.
It is not Adam's guilt that makes us grieve
but innocence upon man's dying tree.

Some Fiery Sea-Dog

As far as I know,
I do not come from a long line of mariners –
at least, not for a thousand years,
but wherever water is, my heart feels at home there,
especially on rivers where the boat's keel
sings under the shadow that clings
like a shoal of minnows, like memories
that never surface, caught in the mind's net.

The lapping of water on a prow
is more comforting than familiar footsteps
down a well-known street, or the beat
felt in the pulse of a hand when words
are hesitant to speak of love.
I think of a river shared in barley-yellow light
when the tide was running with us –
dry land a world we could not trust.

There was another,
where nights were spent in questioning the stars
that teased with their reflections then turned cold
when eyes looked up for answers that surpassed
all calculations of the zodiac.
That river had a guttural chant of voices
rarely silent in my waking hours
and seldom without whispers in the dark.

But even that deep river joins the sea
and there is nothing we can do but let
each current take us at its will
until all tides are one and we belong
where ghosts ride wantonly on waves
that spill their spindrift tears upon the wind.
There I might find a face and recognise at last
the fiery sea-dog who first fathered me.

Marc Harris

The River Beckons for a Last Cast

I wink at you through splinters of starlight
weeds trail like green limbs
and as coracles swirl in your subconscious,
I know I'll pull you in.

So bury me in a creel made of wicker
and make this my last cast.
Drop me in a favourite river,
but do not stand on the bank and weep.

Think of the time we cast a line
on Tywi, Teifi, Taff,
and dream in the reeds where the bittern cries
and swallows sweep flies from the shallows.

And where the river narrows
where the big trout lie,
think fondly of old Dai,
of recollections
swan-white reflections
and foxgloves fingered by bees –

and when the wind breathes
before storm clouds intercede,
maybe, just maybe, I'll sense your soft shoe shuffle.

So bury me in a creel made of wicker
and make this my last cast.
Do not stand on the bank and weep –
I am not dead, but in your sleep.

Note:
A bittern is a scarce heron-like bird, rarely seen. Its cry sounds like a foghorn booming and can be heard up to five kilometres away.

Richard Marggraf Turley

Cursive

The hackwork I leave to others,
malediction my metier,
arms spread to the scene.

May you change from man to woman.

Below on the orange plains,
armies advance from the east,
italicizing our best men.

Let your sky be iron, your earth bronze.

In the outer provinces,
the pen falls into disuse.

May the gods refuse you white bread.

Let your roads be deserted.

May you be violated by donkeys.

Above the trumpets and drums,
may I not be lost for words.

Dylan Jones

Black-out

When I was young, in winter,
my mother rummaged up
the old black-out blanket
extra for my bed – a coarse
brown cloth, like hessian,
marked at every corner
with a hole – where nails went.
And when January lowered
our centigrades & night froze
she pitched on top some
extra coats for thickness
and to soften the chill.
Cosy under this wad of cloth
I juggled my hot Tizer
bottle with thick-socked feet
till it cooled enough for comfort –
Then sleep would jostle in
beside me, settling me down,
inviting me over the threshold
into the lounge of dreams –
So far back! Another time,
another's life like history –
yet it was me – and if the page
were written then the word
was mine, and mine the colours
ranged around me. And this
when I was young, in winter,
stars prickling in the plastic
pond – planets stirruping the hills.

Damian Walford Davies

September Song

from the Welsh of Waldo Williams

The tree of worlds shoots
higher and September
is the space;

the sunstar, ripe and pun-
gent, bows down its
seasoned face.

Under its store of summer
the prime branch
ramifies

through loaded stillness into
our own hearts'
open skies.

And in this border season,
another light
on harm –

at the hub of endless murder
September's sub-
song's calm.

Gerald Wells

Latecomer

…A caul of sky, drawstrung
To the earth's foundations…

     Across two fields
The TV light at Ystrad Ffin goes out…
The last braying politician's been poured
Into his armoured limousine and driven
Into the vanished hills.

       My window sticks
(In Wales rain rains, wood warps),
Yields on a pitch of nipped pig,
And in blunders silence - a hurt man
To his fireside, full of the world,
Dumb with it –
      even to the curling river
I know is there, working its stars
Like rosaries.

     Letting him in,
In tatters and cold,
     I hear nothing…
Hear everything.

Idris Caffrey

A Man on Gwastedyn Hill

Men do not climb mountains
in the hope of meeting someone
but today I share a rock with a stranger
who tells me the story of his life –
he has no intention of listening to mine.

There was so much I could have told him –
how the snow here clings
in the shadows of the valley
long after winter has left the town;
or how kites leave the pine trees
and hover motionless in a racing sky.
If you wait for stars they will always come
and you can just make out down there
the small red house where I was born.

He breaks off at last
and asks me if I'm from around here
but it's just an echo –
he hasn't noticed that I've gone.

Paul Henry

Penllain

In love with an absence
I have wasted my days
believing in this house.

Your limpet ghost clings
to the walls of its rock.
Each night another wave

breaks over you, but you cling
like Gwyneth Blue's painting
and this dust is yours

this sofa where a girl
hugged her knees
and sucked her bony thumb.

Here's where Geta sat,
her old age making profound
the simplest act.

This room's her rockpool still.

Hauling herself up
truth is, she fairly darts
about her element.

There!
She gives the Bush TV a slap.

Where did she flit to then,
her shadow? To what switch,
handle, fabric, utensil?

Ah, she was only pouring tea.
Does china rattle under water?
Does time dart or shuffle?

I'll tilt the blinds
so the sun slides off you.
Forgive me, I have to

get the angle, so you are
always Brown Helen.

I've let in a schoolyard's cries
and birdsong
but louder than these

what the sun says to *Penllain,*
what *Penllain* replies –

Geta? Is that you?
Gwyneth Blue?

Let me read you
'The Song of Solomon'
from Enoch's bible.

Its dark, spineless fossil
lies buried deep on the sil.

Enoch, who begat Geta
who begat Gwyneth Blue
who begat Brown Helen …

Do you mind, Enoch?
It's a bit, you know
ewn but here we go –

'Agorais i'm hanwylyd;
ond fy anwylyd a giliasai,
ac a aethai ymaith …'

The stopped clock translates.

Some brass in the grate,
the doll's head of a broken brush …
Few childhood barnacles remain.

Whose footprints are these
on the sandy floor's mosaic?
They raced through my castle
without disturbing a grain.

Your designer table's
window on a wooden frame
is moored where the piano was.

I am trying to play it now
while drowning in glass.

Dear Brown Helen,
I have wasted my days
believing in a house!

Don't laugh. Oh go on then.
How nonchalantly
your ghost haunts me.

Who were we?
Come back to this sofa
and hug your knees

and suck your bony thumb
and read me
'The Song of Solomon.'

I'll tilt the blinds
so the sun slides off you.

I am a man
come back to this house.

Come back my limpet ghost.

Notes:
st. 19 – ewn – tr. *daring*
st.20 – tr. 'I opened for my lover / but my lover had left;/
he was gone'. (Song of Solomon – Ch. 5 v.6)

The Lichen Gatherer

Make sure the doors to this wood are locked.
Look, here's some moss, or lichen is it
for you. It's wet but it'll soon dry out
like this burnt sienna mud, pocked
and stippled with those who passed through us.

The ghosts of old loves can't find us here.
The rafters leak a little with sky
and, yes, there are too many doors to check
but I think we will be safe here for a while
inside our tangled metaphor.

                                  So smile,
and kiss me, before this moss or lichen dries.

Paul Robichaud

The Spear

after 'Y Gwyayw' by Dafydd ap Gwilym (1320-c.1370)

Beneath her gold-sheened brightness,
I saw a girl – vivacious,
as sprightly as the waves,
golden from head to toe,
day's colour, twice over! –
listening yesterday to
Noah's Ark in the choir
of Deinioel in Bangor.
Enough beauty for the whole
world was there, Fflur's own beauty,
double the pain, a pouring
forth of treason – seeing that
radiant girl! Woe for that gift,
such a severe gash for me!

I was pierced by a seven-
sided spear, know enough grief
for seven songs, and know I
waste away from its poison:
the lust of rivals from Môn.
No man beneath the zodiac
can remove the spearhead from
my heart. It was no blacksmith
who made it, no grinding hand;
its colour, unknown – though fit
for song's praise – nor the weapon's
form, that pierced me, that tamed my
youthful vigour and my looks.

I am driven mad for her,
the candle of Gwynedd! Woe
to me! the shafts long will pierce.
Bless me, but her loveliness
is like Mary's. Sorrowful,
eighteen-fold, my spear-wrought
weakness has made me a sad
lad, with wrinkled cheek: it stings
sharply, care's own skewer.

She with the looks of Essylt
gives it me, the stake in my
bruised breastbone. Wretched to me,
to keep it long, this piercer
of my shattered breast: wasted
cause of pain, love's awl, sorrow's
triple pang, treason's cousin.

Lynn Roberts

Family secrets

Family secrets lie so low, so low
on the quiet paper, gently fading,
foxing; sleeping like a tigerskin,
so still, so low, until you
stir it, poke it, agitate it,
and the fur inflates and the eyes flick
and the mouth yawns with a sudden pink
tongue curl and hedge of fangs.

There in black ink the date, so shy, so shy
on the quiet paper, six years proud of
my birthday year; and the deed poll –
so shy, so secret, changing my
mother's name into my father's;
and I touch it, poke it, agitate it,
and the numbers fire with sudden life,
blazing 'bastard' in foot-high flame.

Family secrets play so dead, so dead
on the quiet page till they are stirred;
till I am reading my mother's life,
so black, so white; she is really Jane Eyre,
the first wife living inconveniently long
in her asylum; I have agitated the past
and the marriage certificate crackles
alive; I am a secret in a Gothic novel.

John Barnie

Swallow

When will I be like the
swallow, he might have said
as we wandered the grounds of
Maindiff Court, costly drugs

dimming his cries to
murmurs; it was dusk, and swallows
dipped for the evening's insects
(nothings that kept them buoyant)

flitting and gliding about our
shoulders, then skimming
the grass where our feet trod;
When will I be like the swallow,

he might have said,
but I'm glad that he didn't;
the evening has gone, and the swallows,
and when I saw him last

under the green mortuary sheet,
the swallows had yet to arrive,
confounding the present
with the past, his lips wiped dry.

The View from Allt-Wen

Seen from the clifftop, crabbers putter flat
against the sea, hooking buoys on deck
and cages; choughs swing out from crevices
with clattering cries just because they can;

there's nothing airy about humans who
do everything to a plan, even the yachters
labouring out of Aberystwyth harbour
planning fun; I suppose the crabs don't know

they're done for in their creepy iron-age
cladding, khaki secateurs snipping at the
light; the choughs have disappeared below my
feet like magicians' apprentices

and water slops against the rocks from
Strumble Head to the blue island mountains of
Pen Llyn; there's nowhere else to go, north,
south, west, or east, this being home.

A Moment of Doubt

When Death was in Patagonia
he spoke Welsh to the few, though
Spanish was more common

and at the end, he said,
language doesn't matter, Arglwydd, or
Dominus from the old days,

the jaw has the last laugh
in any pile of bones, even the animals'
who in life never smiled;

this upset me a bit
as words are important; not so,
Death insisted, only poets

could say that because words are
all they have; leaf through
the Collected Words, has anyone

ever read them except
humans; they don't trouble the stars,
there are no poetry readings on

Mars; I had to agree, yet still…
I'll see you soon, he said; don't bother
writing this down.

Nigel Jenkins

Five Haikus

i

my wet footprint
on the fossilled slab…
extinct within seconds

ii

the daffs that brightened
her memorial bench … long dead
in their colostomy bag

iii

delivered
through the cat-flap – a letter
of moonlight

iv

the tree's final
clutch of leaves – busy, busy
about their slow deaths

v

high tide too
in every dinghy laid up
against the storms

Sheenagh Pugh

How To Leave

Bit by bit. Start at the top
of the Street; work your way along

the little shops, looking, stopping
one last time, as if there were somewhere

you might have missed. At the far end,
where you have to turn down to the harbour,

thinking *was there anything else,* conscious
of turning your back, you feel the first

lurch of loss. But the port is alive
with small boats, trawlers, supply ships;

from the North Ness you can see back over
the whole curve, just before you round

the headland and put it behind you. It gets
no easier; you pause at the museum

to pass some time. An hour goes by
before you know. People have written songs

about leaving this harbour, slow airs
mostly. When you set your face

north again, you are walking toward
the Co-op, and you can tell yourself

you are just out shopping, picking up
a few provisions, but then

you pass the door without going in,
and now what you can see before you

is the ferry terminal. The white ship
squats, its lines unlovely. You board it anyway.

What makes this possible is knowing
you sail out southwards, that the town

has not quite left yet, will be back
briefly, bit by bit, as you go by

leaning on the rail: the museum, the Ness,
the grey town hunched on the hill,

just not for long. Now the harbour
comes in sight; now it is falling

aft; now you round the Knab
and it is gone. However many times

you practise this, it always ends
looking back down a long wake.

Naglfar

They'll be coming to end the world some day,
sicking wolves on to swallow the sun and moon,
stamping crops flat. Their faces slabs of stone,
their eyes tiny. Nothing you can say
will make odds to them; they will not stay
their hand for kindness or reason.
Their fingers snuff stars, not even for fun
but indifferently, along their way

And they will come on the ship Naglfar,
made all of dead men's nails, that cannot sail
until the world has enough of us,
the kind and the cruel both, until the fill
of all those graves takes the shape of our killer,
our leavings at last cobbled into use.

Peter Dale

Blade

Well, you can have your paradise
        if that is what you want.
Go, high above the poor church mice
           and name-worn font,

but let me tell you this, dear sprite:
        if, on some timeless day,
minding your groundless state of light,
          on your boundless way,

you find one blade of real grass pokes
        between two airless thoughts,
you'll yearn for fields of grass and oaks,
         shade of all sorts;

and so you'll take and lay that blade
        between your ideal thumbs,
wanting the reedy note once played,
          but no sound comes,

because that blade grew from my grave
        and I shall be in it,
rooted in earth, nor further crave
         some vapid flit.

Bottles on the Step

Villanelle for my mother

for Georgina Ferry

I seem the only woman under thirty.
      I came away from a soggy farming village.
No hag can say my milk bottles are dirty.

Mutton dressed as lamb, you tittup, flirty.
      You go for smarm and fall for Willy Nillage.
Here I'm the only woman under thirty.

Lips crimson, voice-box like a hurdy-gurdy,
      You couldn't name a finch, mouth made for swillage.
No hag can say my milk bottles are dirty.

Tart, clean your mirror, smirk and watch the birdie,
      Fake fur and knickers notional bits of frillage.
Here, I'm the only woman under thirty.

You couldn't tell what's cledge and what is cherty.
      Digging in nails is all you know of tillage.
No hag can say my milk bottles are dirty.

You old gate-legs, your husband's always shirty,
      Your blokes, leftovers of a rapeseed spillage.
You seem the only tart here double thirty.
No hag can say my milk bottles are dirty.

Nonsuch Park; Easter Island

Hardwood's the best all-weather timber.
Well made with brass memorial plaques,
the headstone benches stare at winter
in this and a thousand parks.

New benches, built to thwart the vandals,
glint their names across the grass.
More seats than seated in green rectangles
wait for winter to pass.

They watch for Primavera, the goddess,
her equable spring – or Eastertide.
– Villages by the logged rain-forest
dregs in the mud-slide.

Roland John

Looking for Elpenor

How then to enter the place of no return,
search out the ferryman or Avernus' gate
when maps are faulty, the geography
unknown or obscure and the way strait?

And yet the heroes found the path,
across dark seas, passed through the fire
to come to the biddable place unexpected;
where now the guides once readily for hire?

Is it through books that one finds the river?
Dante's sleep or waking alone to find
that unfriendly shore with Satters and Pulley
gazing at the terrible city that calls our kind.

History traces back to that first intellect
with Odysseus sent to discover and ask
those questions we query still, wary of
detecting, yet he understood the task.

So here as with the dreams that matter
yet relate to no reality, nor confidence,
the entrance beckons and with a little
weariness our crossing can commence.

Love Song

Here at the edge of things,
the quarry's rim, a turn of trees,
with you below calling out.

The susurrus through branches
dumbs you, your arms flail
as you semaphore some meaning.

The sun deadens my interest,
the wind's whisper is intriguing
I am oblivious to your gestures.

Once they would have set me
running down the perilous track
enticed and bewildered.

Neither time nor space
have altered; rather the changes
are appropriate to us

who seldom understood the clues,
those connections that snap,
a tightness embraced

this is where we have reached,
washed up, contented,
resigned to small delights.

Peter Finch

The Death of Phil Ochs

Vietnam at its peak Ochs reached Cardiff
played the old red-brick student's union
before they pulled it down.
A church full of slim-jeaned hipsters
polo-necked beards.
It was their war not our war the
bombs of others their blood their fire.
Tet and Mai Lai and Nixon's
peace with honor a thousand miles away.
Didn't stop us wanting our protesting heard.
Ochs came on to cheering I Ain't
Marching This is the Land of The Power and
the Glory did The Bells and The Highwayman twice
had us on our feet did them again
life in his eyes like electricity
the demons of doubt and the
the fear of failure yet to burn.
Took six more years until
the war was over and the bipolar raging
ran in his veins enough to wreck him.
Hung himself at his sister's home
in Far Rockaway NY. Lamé suit in
the case. No gold records on the wall.

Out in the street after the union gig. By the train tracks.
Lines to the coal. Ochs his hands in his pockets. On his own.
Went for a curry. God what a south Wales thing.
Talked about guitar chords and Minnesota
and his friend his not friend Bob
and a bit about lithium and the way the sun always rose.
Didn't mention pain or death. Next gig somewhere north
of here. Just a walk up the road. Didn't mention
death at all.

Kathy Miles

Skeletons in the Cupboard

Newport, 2006

Boat-buried, his skull smashed
under the hull of a medieval ship.
His ribs entwined with hers, seawashed,
a riddle of bones and wood. Robust, muscular,
he once held his woman tight, carried fire
home in his arms, fetched food and kindling.

Skeletons under the landscape move
in the swell of waves. A cradle of sand rocks
clavicle or femur, a pelvic girdle turning to coral.
In my hand might be shells, or the crushed
shards of his spine. A polished disk, slipped
inside the mouth of a man who died
defending his fort, or harvesting the wheat.

A shine in the slid-back tide shows white
against the water. He was slurried here in the salt rush
of the estuary, riding the bore at a full moon
under a hundred bridges from the marsh,
sliding beneath the sterns of many ships
until he rested, among the chips of bowl and cannon shot.

And here now are the confident seamen,
Their bold hands full of boat, easing the sheets,
fixing a halyard or genoa, shackles gleaming grease.
Going home to a hot shower, to a roundhouse of brick
and steel. But above on the hill, they are still his sheep,
last of their line, grazing fat and lazy, good Welsh mutton.

Swans

Once, you were slippery and warm with me.
Held tightly in the membrane of your arms,
I don't remember that careful holding,
the blanket tucked beneath the edge of my breathing.
In my past head you are smiling
as we walk together on the beach.
I see a cotton sling of deckchairs,
hear my father's easy laugh.
You in the blue gingham skirt,
your dark hair whipped with salt.

Even then we were building houses.
White stones for doors and windows,
razor-shells for the drawbridge.
Sea ate away at flimsy walls
as you battled to keep the structure.
Sand folded by the crush of tide,
like sheets we squared between us in the wash.
Drawing runes on the beach,
and I was always the smallest,
dwarfed by shadows of the sun,
the planet-roundness of your body.

Yesterday, I saw my christening gown.
Tucked into tissue, carefully wrapped,
it served both of us well, and long before that,
your mother, too. I marvel at the stitching,
the chain that links three generations.
Each parting-time we hug polite goodbyes,
and threads are drawn apart a little further.
I see myself, once helpless in your arms,
tugging at the pale mound of your breast.
As you're now helpless in a silent bond
that makes us swim, like two mute swans,
round and round in the circle of this water.

Philip Williams

Castell y Bere

Lost in a long valley it melts
like a pill on its tongue of rock,
dissolves into secret, shy defiance
behind a surcoat skirt of screening trees.

That sort of boy, we sought it out,
drawn by the dull bass of its drum towers,
disappointed how little there was to see
after our damp nights on those sour hills.

Returning after many years I found
my memory wanting. More there now
than met the eye. More than the low
remembered ramparts, the view

of Craig yr Aderyn, Cader's perpetual frown
and the determined, D-shaped towers folded
to form an empty fist. The most prominent of them
rode proud as a prow as though to part the sea.

We looked back from its deck along its waist and stern.
One soft voice lilting, settling incessantly on the penultimate
stress, spoke of Llewellyn, how well he had lived.

A boy from the south country, sharing after seven centuries
the sonority of the language, little of its sense,
I agreed, admired with him the emperor's old clothes.

Return to Catterick

Men went to *Catraeth*, keen their war-band; pale mead their portion, it was poison.
Three hundred under orders to fight and, after celebration, silence.
Though they went to churches for shriving, true is the tale, death confronted them.
From *Y Gododdin*, Aneirin c.600 AD. Translated by Joseph Clancy.

You always wanted to return
to the place you'd cried yourself to sleep
your first night away from home.

Drilling in the drizzle of a parade-ground square
you'd found your feet, found your aim,
formed an enduring fondness for beer.

You always wanted to return.
We discussed it in bars, in my back room,
your vague plan to visit Yorkshire once again,
where I had followed so much later,
to study not to march, to study and had stayed.

'Men went to Catraeth,' to feed
black ravens on the wall of the fort,
to slaughter and were slain.
I knew Aneirin from the anthologies,
the archaeology of an unlearned language.
'Men went to Catraeth,' paid for their poison
and after celebration, silence.

Shipped to Cyprus, Suez,
the edge of empire's last small wars,
marriage, two sons, assisted passage
('Ten Pound Poms'), divorce –
you never did return to Catterick
to realise your final promise.

For your heart called time and stopped
like a clock on your last Cornish holiday.
And at your committal in our common valley
your second family and your first
did not dare to play *Gwa Hoddiad*,
lest everybody cry.

Robert Minhinnick

In the Gŵli

i

Salo?
Requiem for a Dream?
They were all there.
Schoolchildren had kicked open a box
in my neighbour's garage. Out had fallen
the cartridges and soon in the gwli
behind our house those hours of torture
were turned into miles of videotape.

ii

Amongst the vodka bottles and the nipplewort,
around the broken guttering and through love-in-a-mist,
that trail gleamed black. How the boys laughed
as they tied the girls with Cannibal Holocaust.
How the girls shivered in their carbon ropes.

iii

I looked up. The monsoon was mauve.
Every molecule of that rain. And there was more of it
to come. But for some reason I was out and about,
a few Monday walkers with me, all now sure
to be betrayed by weather not predictable,
weather beyond us and our experience of Mondays
or any day in the new world of weather.

iv

But who cared about rain?
Not I. Because they were there.
And then they were not there.
A black chaff around the stacks,
their flight unspooling like videotape
about those limestone stooks.

v

Choughs, I said.
The woman looked alarmed.
Choughs, I shouted, and on she strode,
away from the madman's weather.
They're choughs, I laughed after her.
So this is our chance. To be charged with choughs.

vi

What was I but a dog barking in the rain,
watching my sky burn like a tapestry,
a southern sky charred by choughs,
each chough a chalice filled with ashes,
each chough a choice of life, of death.
For there come days when we can choose.
And I chose choughs.

vii

She made off to the lifeguard's telephone
in its yellow box. Now that was a weapon
I had wondered at. I pictured a saint's bones
in its pyx, one million surveillance cameras
pointed at an empty street.

viii

Listen, please. If these are the words,
I have to use them. After all,
though the sky is radiant with language,
I take no credit. And should I feel shame
for chattering of choughs? Should I apologise?
It was my first time. And such glossy tumblers.
Guerrillas of anti-gravity.
One had even touched down
and with its red awl was testing the turf.

ix

No, I thought. Because thinking is safer
than speaking. There are not enough choughs.
Not here. Not here in the rain. Not here
in the rain with Silence of the Lambs
around my ankles. Not enough choughs
to go round. Not enough to redeem us now.
Not enough choughs to challenge ourselves.

x

Soon, I thought, they will arrive to put me away.
An undigital man who chawed of choughs.
Who called this cliff a church of choughs.
Which are gone. Yes, the choughs have shuffled off.
But soon the search party will arrive.
And the dogcatcher with his net.

Steven O'Brien

The Coral Rosary

Tonight I shout my sister down
From wet slate, balcony and parapet,
Pitch her name against iron railings,
To make her cold tongue ring again.

I clamour deserted alleys,
Trammel flooded gutters,
Like hammering a pewter tray-
Gull woken ruck. Reel and soak.

The department store window is black water –
A standing mere
Spanned by mullion, arch and sill.

My face is lava-lamped in neon
And she is there,
My sister in the deep,
Chromed across a mannequin –
Synching her lips with mine.

I star my fingers
Across the glisten lip of a hanging tarn
Yet there is no tug of current. No hand drag.

A scant fathom down
And pale as a marsh taper
She grieves the joints
Of her numb fingers
Like saying a coral rosary –

Each mimed white bead
Tells how she is finds herself now in glint shards –

A room's hoarse cough
With its door just slammed.
The glanced edge of my look away eye
In the bathroom mirror.

She reaches
But I touch only plate-thrum.
I cannot delve the platen's chill veneer.
She cannot pass the glass gate.

When I turn my back
There are no stifled cries.
Just one mute tap –
Like the poc of a calor gas flame.

The road home is a glimmer fen –
Street lights barely flex on each new pool.
I stoop and glimpse the fish-bone sliver
Of a clipper moon repeated.

The Gates of Paradise

A morning in paradise.
Cain listens at the gates
Tropically naked
Thick as shit.

He swings on the mute lock,
Fingers the greased hinges,
Palms the deep wood,

Then puts his lips
To a row of nails
Pursing on one loose iron nipple,

Which he tongues hard –
Pushing the loose spike until it falls
To chime exactly
On the earth outside.

He looks through the hole.

There hangs the moon.

He has never seen it before.

Wind
Like the fleet kiss
Of a serpent's fork.

Wind
Like a white dream-shirt
On his bare shoulder.

He grinds against the cold latch –
Begins to work his dumb sprung cock
Into a mandrake stump.

He tastes
Dark lees blood
On a woman's thigh.

He hears
A baby's torn moans
Cloying through rubble.

Now he screws his eye,
Sees nothing –
Only rangy jackals

Sand and corpses
Under a scythe of stars.

Yet Cain,
Like a teenage shelf-stacker
With his first witless hard-on
Wants it anyway.

And as he burnishes himself
To a sudden amazement.

The bolts draw back
The doors scrape open,
His seed lashes
Into the night.

Wendy Holborow

A Rose-Coloured Italian Afternoon

Vivace   A glockenspiel of laughter spills into the sultry stillness
of the hilled city, sucks us into its slipstream.

A spider spins our hopes on a gossamer harp.
Vague memories hang around like cobwebs.

Rose Rhapsody, Symphony, Distant Thunder.

Arpeggio   Invisible cicadas on fruiting lemon trees rasp
like a bow-scratch boy fretting over his scales.

Forte   Kettledrum thunder bounces quadraphonic sounds
from the mountains which surround the city.

The drumming rain drowns the laughter.
Pizzicato   Plucks our hopes. Staccatos the cicadas.

*

Adagio   For the sake of the giddy-fragrant rose the rain must water the thorns,
its pain contained under a spreading plane tree in the piazza
where we pause on old stone steps, worn and crumbled by feet long
vanished.
Articulate bells ring from the campanile and we are smitten by sounds
and smells.

September Song, Bright Melody, Lyric.

Sky's the Limit
A capella   An eagle splits the sky.

Pianissimo Tears of joy
and tears of bitterness
will water roses.

Hybrid, Climbing, Rambling.

Dissonance	We battle in a bee-loud garden against
	greenfly, mildew, fungus, black spot.
	Bumblebees bully the crimson mouths
	of the roses and rob them of their nectar.
Largo	Deadheading: dreams scatter from our hands as we offer
	the petals to Zephyrus who zithers their flight.
	Floribunda, Grandiflora,
	Old English, (transplanted into foreign soil, dewdrops like sobs)
Expressivo	But the fragrance stays in the hand that gives the rose
	so we gather armfuls for our friends
	avoiding thorns we dream of unicorn horns
	of magic briars, of sleeping princesses.

*

Finale	Now, the rainfall is as quiet as a conductor
	turning the page, the whisper of a flute.
	Our rose-tinted lives played out like a musical score
	on several staves at the same time.
Coda	We strain to hear the laughter again,
	as the last rose petal falls.

Richard Gwyn

Translation

All your stories are about yourself, she said, even when they
seem to be about other people. I was not going to deny this, nor
give her the pleasure of being right. So I quoted Proust, who
said that writers don't invent books; they find them within
themselves and translate them. This seemed to do the trick, and
she fell silent. I dipped my fingers into a bowl of scented water
and started on the rice. An aftertaste of clay and leaves and
metal took me by surprise. What is in this rice? I asked her.
Mushroom stock? Shotgun cartridge? Earthworm? No, she said,
peering at me through the candlelight, the stories that you
haven't written yet are in the rice. You must be tasting them.

Lone Rider

How old he seemed in the dusk – how he smarted and burned
inside and smiled and rolled his cigarette, reading the
international news, committed now to a patching up of lives, the
construction of bridges, a resolve to still the cries of orphans. In
the past few years, vague anxieties had pressed upon him like
the attentions of a nervous dog worrying his ankles. He had been
in the Balkans and knew the counting of bodies, but still was
not prepared for this. He saw the bloated corpses riding on the
waters of the flooded river; he counted the cost of lives in
hundreds and in thousands. He was glutted with the distress of
other people. But more: he was witness to the disintegration of
others' memories, puzzled by collective amnesia as much as
actual genocide. His idea of God was re-awakened, ironically,
by an earthly oppression he could no longer serve, or even
acknowledge. There was a wilderness inside him that was more
terrifying than anything he had encountered in his years as war
correspondent, evangelist, murderer, thief of souls; he needed to
contain that wilderness, to channel it into his thin fingers, let it
scorch everything he touched. At the same time, he saw himself
as a perfectly respectable horseman riding out one fine May
morning across the fields of Connemara.

Vagrant

She wanders miraculously sane through the old port, looking for a safe place to sleep. *Best to hang out in a gang, if you're a girl.* Alice despises gangs. She would rather risk being alone, although it scares her. She sings a song, *a knife, a fork, a bottle and a cork*, yes she sings that, and she carries a knife, a bottle and a blanket. She walks quickly, eyes focused ahead. She needs to focus because stopping is not an option. She finds an abandoned warehouse, a place she has slept before. She climbs dangerous stairways to a room with broken windows. She peers out onto the quay. Cranes hang like tall sentries over the ships. Everything is corroded by sea-water and neglect and smells of rust and diesel. She settles in the furthest corner of the room, takes a candle stub from her pocket and lights it. She folds herself in her blanket and props herself against the wall. She sucks strong coarse wine from the bottle. The taste makes her want to gag, but the warmth is in her blood now. She takes the letter from her pocket, flattens it on her knee, and begins to read for the third time that day. *My darling Alice, By the time you read this I will be shooting up rainwater. I hope you suffer, as I have suffered on account of you . . .* She smiles and holds the corner of the letter over the candle flame.

September Night

From my window I watch a train as it leaves the brightly-lit station, just across the river. Rain falls heavily, splintering the glare of street-lamps. Elgar, whose music I do not care for, attempts a seduction. I admire the visual articulation of a particular row of books in the corner of this book-crammed room. A rubber plant bursts up between the banister and a box of files. The cello glides uncanny in the flame of a candle, cantering now, along a receding tide, astute to the melancholy of the boy I was, catch me catch me, bury me in the solitude of dusk and I will waken one week later badder and wilder than before. A click on the tape-deck reminds me that the concerto has come to an end. Cars slosh through the street below. I open the skylight a little higher and cool night air invades my room. Another train pulls out, hauling drunks to Merthyr after a day on the lash, this one's on me boys, and the rain falls on the railtrack and the road and the houses and the river as I put on my mask and prepare for the first guest of the night.

Keith Jones

Prayers

thirty nine
three covens of you
three circlings of the years
about three crumpling continents
& today
on the spiral's axis
as we two
lean into one twisting future
may we love
being into being

let there be
a slow cauldron of calm
let the days
that crackle & splutter beneath it
be worlds we spoke
& let the figures
achant on its rim
their thumbs & little fingers throbbing
be wild
in red eyed grace

in your own spaces
let the wind fetch
clean clouds
that you may stay
gentle

Diyarbakr

(Turkey)

diyarbakr was old
when the romans were new
in this treacleblack stone, this slow
basaltic sludge stared at
by poppies,
exfoliating in
40 degrees Celsius

scorpion old

& in the hills the heroes,
on their backs too
a swollen sting,
dosed up with heroin they
grimace as they bit
into green
exploding peppers

dreaming the university of night

raki clouding at twatlight
the cockstrut of soldiers
holding hands, sniffing roses,
about them the cells
of goldsmiths, silver shapers,
tinbeaters, flyswarming meatsellers
cobblers gobbling nails

all this old as Tamberlaine

& now the neon windows
the orange
negligées, the pavilions of Paris
the petals opened for you
the desperation
like heads in a plastic bag
hearts like birds searching for windows

old as the conquest of someone else's woman.

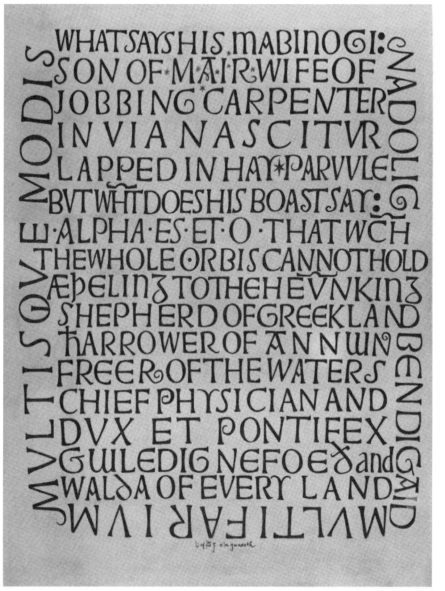

Fig. 1   Inscription by **David Jones**

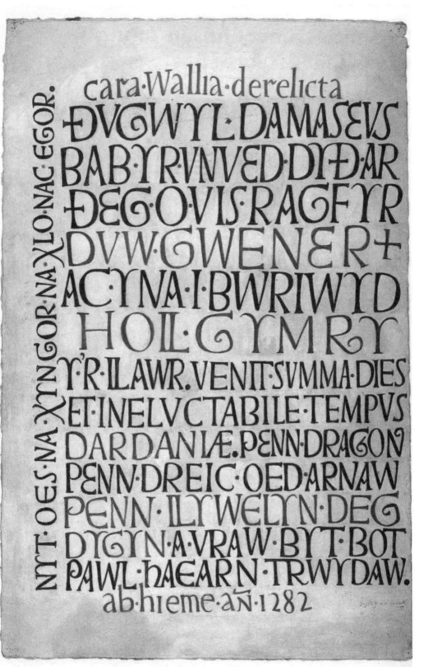

cara·Wallia·derelicta

ÐVGWYL·DAMASEVS
BAB·YRVNVED·DIÐAR
ÐEG·OVIS·RAGFYR
DVW·GWENER✝
AC·YNA·I·BWRIWYD
HOIL·GYMRY
Y'R·ILAWR·VENIT·SVMMA·DIES
ET·INELVCTABILE·TEMPVS
DARDANIÆ·PENN·DRAGON
PENN·DREIC·OED·ARNAW
PENN·ILYWELYN·DEG
DYGYN·A·VRAW·BYT·BOT
PAWL·HAEARN·TRWYDAW.
ab·hieme·añ·1282

NYT·OES·NA·XYN·GOR·NA·XLO·NAC·EGOR.

Fig. 2   Inscription by **David Jones**

80

Tim Smith-Laing: Chosen Young Broadsheet Essayist

Tim Smith-Laing was born in 1985 and grew up in Kent. In 2004 he was named one of the Foyle Young Poets of the Year, and later that year started a BA in English Literature at Pembroke College Cambridge. Having graduated in 2007, he is currently studying for a master's degree at Balliol College, Oxford, while pursuing his writing and photography. His photographs have appeared in *JPEG Magazine*, and his poetry has been published in *Agenda Broadsheet* and the *Tower Poets* anthology.

'My Greek Sailors Speak Cockney':

The principle of abstraction in a selection of the works of David Jones

i

Jones' poetics and their background

Though this essay restricts itself substantially to analysis of the written work, one cannot separate Jones' background in visual art from his literary thinking, and to say 'poetics' is in no way to do so. I follow Jones himself in using 'poetic' in the very strictest sense, as regarding *poiesis*, making. From his letters and essays, it is clear that Jones viewed *poiesis* as an all-encompassing definition of art, consistently applying 'making' to any artistic project. As he says of the 'making of a writing' in 'Autobiographical Talk', 'I regard this water-colour which I have just completed as belonging *im*plicitly [sic] to the same world ... as that to which *The Anathémata* belongs',[1] because the two fall under the same banner as all the other 'gratuitous', 'extra-utile' and 'intransitive' activities, defined as *poieses*, which lend man the 'unique title [of] *poeta*'.[2] Rather than viewing what we so often call 'the arts' as separate activities, Jones sees them merely as different media for the same activity; making is making, regardless of whether the means of production be graphic, linguistic, performative, or some mixture of the three. Poetry, painting, carving are only as different as oil paint and watercolour; media used as befits their suitability to the task at hand and the artist's competence. As Harman Grisewood writes,

> [Jones] would talk of the problems of picture making or writing simply as though they were those of a structural engineer, calculating whether this chosen material would in fact bear that particular thrust of meaning[3]

and it is this awareness of the exigencies and limitations of media as well as his own aptitudes that guides Jones' output. Paint, pencil, ink and words are simply the various 'species' [4] under which his thoughts find expression.

Just as all arts are drawn together by their being gratuitous *poiesis*, so are they drawn together by the aim of that *poiesis*: the creation of form. For Jones, it is the 'form-creating quality'[5] of an action that defines it as the creation of an artwork. It is this that draws together the arguments of 'Art in Relation to War' and 'Art and Sacrament': art, war and sacraments are considered analogous because of their formal aspects; the 'delight' of form draws Rommel's desert tactic and 'Nelson's Nile touch' together with Norman vaulting and Piero della Francesca's *Nativity*.[6] This delight and illuminating power of form, 'the *splendor formae* of St Thomas',[7] leads us to Jones' Neo-Platonism, and to Maritain's *Art et Scholastique*: the reference is a direct echo of the Maritain text that is so crucial to understanding Jones' thinking.

Already attracted by post-impressionist art theory on his return from war, with Clive Bell's talk of 'Significant form ... [as] the one quality common to all works of visual art',[8] Jones' philosophy was very much in its 'sap years' when he came across Maritain's contextualization of similar ideas in a Catholic setting – drawing together the two most important preoccupations of Jones' life, his art and his adopted religion. The Thomist conception of art expounded in *Art et Scholastique* is inescapable in Jones' writing.[9]

Maritain upholds the prime importance of significant form, writing of 'the sensible signs of art',[10] the 'subordination of the matter to the light of the form'[11] and '"*forma*" ... [as] the principle which upbuilds and completes all things in their essence and in their qualities'.[12] The primacy of form then leads to a recognition of the necessity of admitting artworks to be artworks rather than aspiring to make '*servile and abject copies* of nature'.[13] As such, one of the definitive qualities of an artwork is its *otherness*, the degree to which it is no longer simply that which it is made of, nor an imitation of its subject, but an effective sign of that subject and a significant form in and of itself. For Jones, the artist 'deals wholly in signs',[14] creating them from the *materia* to hand. He illustrates the point, deliberately choosing a representational work, Hogarth's *Shrimp Girl*, stating '[it is] as they say "faithful to the appearance of nature", [but truly it is] a *signum* of that reality, under the species of paint', an 'objective sign'.[15]

It is this that leads us to the notion of abstraction, for as Jones states, however well the sign may call forth the 'reality' that it intends to, that reality is never '"really present" in the particular sense used by theologians'.[16] 'The ontological separation of a work of art from its object', as Dilworth sums up in regard to Jones, 'is prerequisite to the work's being a symbol'.[17] It is just this separation that Jones seems to understand as the essential meaning of abstraction when he writes that:

> Those of us whose work no one, I imagine, would call 'abstract', know, nevertheless, that it is an abstract quality, however hidden or devious, which determines the real worth of any work. This is true of Botticelli's *Primavera*, of the White Horse of Uffington, of the music of Monteverdi, of *Finnegans Wake* of the 'Alfred Jewel', of the glass goblet I am now trying to draw, of the shape of a liturgy, of the shape of a tea-cup[18]

As the letter continues, Jones distinguishes between this necessary principle without which 'a "thing" having integration and life of its own could not be' and what is termed ' "abstract art" '. That genre, so carefully isolated in inverted commas, relies on 'the assertion , in isolation, of a real, and indeed a first, principle'.[19] Fifteen years later, Jones would call the 'restrictive use' of the term 'regrettable because misleading'.[20] Regrettable because misleading, and misleading because it places abstraction as antithetical to 'realistic' representation, an approach that Jones consistently refutes as, at best, oversimplification.

ii

The principle in action

The fact that realism and abstraction cannot be considered antithetical is key to the integration of *In Parenthesis*. The apparently documentary content of the poem could be taken for strict realism, and the more evidently allusive passages for some form of literary abstraction – perhaps the 'romantic associative' of 'Religion and the Muses'.[21] However, when Jones writes to Renée Hague that 'How to make it not *realistic* is the bugger',[22] he is not talking of doing so via the supperaddition of the romantic elements, nor their more subtle fusion to the poem, but something deeper again.

To take the apparently naturalistic direct speech of the poem for example: the night patrol of Part 3 is littered with snippets of cockney phrasing and phonetics, from 'cushy mate', to 'you all right china? – lift us yer rifle', but on closer inspection, Jones does not reproduce every nuance *ad absurdum*. One paragraph faithfully begins with the dropped H and V-for-'th' of 'Nuvver 'ole mate…look where yer going', (p.39) but elsewhere 'hole' retains its H despite being direct speech (p.36) with cockney around it; nor is 'going' reduced to 'goin' or glottal-stops noted in words such as 'halted'. As Dilworth states in his discussion of the poem's genre (*Shape of Meaning*, Chapter 2), much of the cockney speech that appears time and again is far from straightforwardly mimetic. He notes that where early drafts 'faithfully reproduced Cockney … [recalling] the ludicrous colloquial speech of Kipling's verse',[23] the final version of the poem 'diminish[es] orthographical notation of Cockney pronunciation while preserving … syntax, rhythms, and vocabulary' and creates a 'language … only suggestive of Cockney'.[24]

This diminution, Dilworth suggests, 'sustains intimacy' with the reader, and gives a 'closer approximation of the effect of reality';[25] I would contend that over and above these things, the aim is to aid the integration of the poem's different *materia*. In Jones' letter above, the problem of 'how not to make it realistic' follows from the difficulty of how to make a 'real enduring shape'.[26] Making the speech not 'embarrassing',[27] while keeping its essential character, preserves its incarnational effectiveness, its ability to re-present the *effect* of the actual cockney speech heard by Jones, without the ludicrousness of absurd pedanticism distracting us from our experience of the poem as a whole, a shape, 'a thing having integration and a life of its own'. Moreover, though the subtle abstraction of the poem's direct speech is certainly an attempt to come closer to the effect of the reality behind it, the other abstractions of poem, contrary to Dilworth's other suggestion, counteract intimacy. The heightened linguistics continually alert the reader to 'the careful punctuation and slight specialness'[28] that Jones sees in the writing he admires. The density of prose and poetry in *In Parenthesis* is intensely involving, but not intimate, for intimacy implies an ease of communication that Jones' poetry avoids.

Being alerted to this, however, draws one down into the weave of the poetry, looking for secondary significances. Colin Wilcockson demonstrates the effectiveness of Jones' technique in his essay 'David Jones and the Waste-Land Motif'. Analysing a passage from Part 4, he notes the variety of tonal register covered in just a single page, from the ordered military terminology, to the hints of nursery-rhyme, to 'a particular kind of formality', which I associate with the 'slight specialness' referred to above. Further, he states, one finds in that last mode a 'sacramental *Untertext*'. [29]

Wilcockson's analysis needs no repeating, and bears out its contention convincingly; but what is important here is that Jones' modulations of tone, the shaping of the text itself, rather than overt reference, lead one to look deeper and further. In abstracting the language from the natural, it becomes evident to the reader that the text is not only representational of the primary subject, but of a secondary subject as well. However the secondary – or rather coexistent – significance is, in the words of Maritain, 'spontaneous and intuitively grasped, not hieroglyphic'.[30] Abstraction from the natural points us to search deeper; and via the desire to perform that search we recognise the weight of the passage's significance, even if hieroglyphic translation fails us.

The same is true of passages from the section of *The Book of Balaam's Ass* published in *The Sleeping Lord and Other Fragments*. The soldiers' names range from the apparently mundane 'Bell' and 'Jack Smart', to the evidently romantic-associative reference to Malory's ill-fated brother-knights in 'signaller Balin and his incompatible mess-mate linesman Balan', to the almost jokingly loaded 'Private Lucifer'.[31] This range alerts the reader to the possibility of secondary readings, so that when we come to

'Corporal Oliver of No. 1 nor for
Corporal Amis and
Lance Corporal Amile of No. 2' [32]

we are struck by the oddness of 'Amile' appearing as an English name, and then further struck by the different ways of reading all three names. Oliver recalls us to *Le Chanson de Roland* and Jones' statement in the preface to *In Parenthesis* that in the early part of the war 'Roland could find, and, for a reasonable while, enjoy, his Oliver'.[33] Amis then becomes patient of being read as the English name, as 'amiss' – recalling the 'by misadventure' of the dedication to *In Parenthesis* – and more importantly, as the French *amis*, with its weighted connotations from *In Parenthesis*. Finally Amile contains within it the possibility of 'a *miles* ', and Jones'

84

fascination with the idea of *Christus miles*, which appears later in the fragment when the soldiers 'call strongly from their several and lonely places' on

'the Son of Mary, because, like Perédur, He left
His Mother to go for a soldier, for he would be a *miles* too.' [34]

In *The Anathémata*, the abstract nature of the poetry is far more evident – the title of this essay is one of Jones' notes to the poem, embracing with gusto the idea of making 'it not realistic'. Indeed, the poem's title itself – of which I am anxious to preserve the cover's accented *é* – has to do with the concept of abstraction. The accent marks a distinction between the transliterations of the Greek words ἀναθήματα and ἀναθέματα, where the difference between the long *epsilon* and short *eta* divides the various meanings the word has inhabited. As Jones states in his preface:

I knew that…*anathema* (spelt with an epsilon) meant (firstly) something holy but that in the N.T. it is restricted to the opposite sense [of cast out, cursed]. While this duality fitted my requirements, the English word 'anathemas', because referring only to the opposite sense, was of no use to me … however … there was the other English plural, 'anathemata', meaning devoted things, … preserving in our language the ancient and beneficent meaning; for 'anathemata' comes from *anathema* spelt with an eta of which the epsilon form is a variant.[35]

In a move typical of his encyclopaedic and inclusive mind, Jones then states that he means by the title

the blessed things that have taken on what is cursed and the profane things that somehow are redeemed: the lights and also the 'ornaments', both in the ordinary sense of gear and paraphernalia and in the sense of what simply adorns; the donated and votive things, the things dedicated after whatever fashion, the *things in some sense made separate* [my italics] being 'laid up from other things'; things, or some aspect of them that partake of the extra-utile and of the gratuitous; things that are the signs of something other.[36]

So it is that anathémata define themselves in the order of artworks, partaking of the same 'extra-utile' and 'gratuitous' quality. Moreover, the term not only contains that same notion of ontological separation as abstraction does, its etymology also recognises the danger of the abstract being not that which is separate by virtue of self-integration, but that which is separate through being cast-out or exiled.

This threatening sense of abstraction hangs over Jones' poetry. His particular preoccupations leave him unwilling, and even unable, to write in terms of references widely recognisable to readers whom 'centuries and centuries of cultural metamorphoses'[37] separate from the literary deposits of the ages. His recognition of such is ever-present in his concern for the 'validity' of his work, his provision of extensive and encyclopedic notes, and more importantly in the subject matter of the poetry itself. The performers of 'known-site ritual frolics' in 'The Tutelar of the Place' become modern artists in attempting to

> laud and magnify with made, mutable and beggarly elements the unmade immutable begettings and precessions of fair-height, with halting sequences and unresolved rhythms, searchingly, with what's to hand, under the inconstant lights that hover world-flats, that bright by fit and start the tangle of world-wood, rifting the dark drifts for the wonderers that wind the world-meander … seeking hidden grammar to give back anathema its first benignity.[38]

The description of poetry contained in 'halting sequences and unresolved rhythms' is subject to an anxious humility, as is the description of the poet's *materia* as 'made, mutable and beggarly elements' and 'what's to hand' in sharp contrast to the 'unmade immutable begettings and precessions' they hope to laud.

The anxiety of the search for means to 'give back anathema its first benignity' is a recognition of the comment on the position of art in the modern world that is contained in the duality of the term. Jones' fear that the position of *poiesis* – artistic and religious – in the modern world falls far more easily under the malign sense of anathema is clear. He saw the modern world as facing an imminent, perilous 'break' between itself and its creations, in an age where technology was perfecting *praxis* – doing – at the price of the near death of *poiesis*,[39] casting out art in the process. As he states in a letter to the Bollingen Foundation in 1959,

> [all artists must be] whether they know it or not, whether they would repudiate the notion or not, … "showers forth" of things which tend to be impoverished, or misconceived, or altogether lost or wilfully *set aside* [my italics] in the preoccupations of our present intense technological phase[40]

Otherwise mankind risks a permanent and irrevocable anathema, an abstraction of a kind far distant from the abstraction of a thing having 'integration and life of its own': the break between mankind and the sign-making activity that, to Jones' mind, is its defining characteristic.[41]

Everywhere, alongside its well-explored theological and historical content, *The Anathémata* is filled with illustration and justification of this ideology. So sharp is the threat that in the poem's opening the agents of 'the break' and those opposing it are metaphorically militarised: the priest and his company become

> These rear-guard details in their quaint attire, heedless of incongruity, unconscious that the flanks are turned and all connecting files withdrawn or liquidated – that dead symbols litter to the base of the cult-stone, that the stem by the palled stone is thirsty, that the stream is very low.

'The utile infiltration nowhere held
creeps vestibule
is already at the closed lattices, is coming through each door.'[42]

As our mytho-symbolic vocabulary becomes 'impoverished' or wilfully disregarded, our symbols die, the cultural stream dries up, the 'utile' quality that defines doing as opposed to making takes over. The hopelessness of the situation is summed up by the coldly formal evocation of the old song's 'They're coming through the window...', used too in one of the darkest moments of *In Parenthesis*.[43] Nearly entirely cut off from hope of rescuing his situation, 'The cult man', both priest and artist, 'stands alone in Pelham's land', both the literal wasteland of Malory's *Morte d'Arthur* and the Eliot-inflected cultural waste land of the modern age.

The bridging imperative of the Bollingen statement is enacted in the poem's continuous search for links from prehistory to history to the present. Asking of the 'new-born shapes' of the 'Middle-Sea and Lear-Sea' section 'Are the proto-forms already ours?',[44] Jones edges toward stating that they are, as well as implicitly insisting with 'we' that he and his readers are a unit, having a shared cultural past that *we* must comprehend. When the proto-forms become Greek sculpture and he asks of 'the Delectable Korê'

> is she Elêne Argive
> or is she transalpine Eleanore
> or our Gwenhwyfar
> the Selenê of Thulê

Jones is delving deep into the probability that all three are versions and mutations of the one same archetypal 'Virgo Potens'. As he explores it in his essay 'The Viae': 'The truth is that whether we are Greeks or barbarians, Celts or Romans or whoever we are, we cannot for long suppose a creativity without the female principle'.[45] The intersections between Celtic and Classical history that he cites above demonstrate that truth in action, both etymologically and historically, in the mutations that link Elêne to Eleanore, to Gwenhwyfar, to Selenê .

There is more to be explored in the other instances of this bridging that are to be found throughout *The Anathémata* (and throughout *The Sleeping Lord*), but it is the point where the anxiety of Jones' concern with abstraction meets its formal aspect that is most interesting. In subtitling the poem as *fragments of an attempted writing*, he recognises his failure to complete, to have made *a* shape.[46] There's no doubting that the fragments are very finely shaped internally, but in still remaining, to Jones' mind, fragmented from one another, the book is not a whole. However, he states that 'If it has a shape it is chiefly that it returns to its beginning',[47] and though this seems by-the-by, it is a vital reaction against the linearity of traditional narrative, a reaction which can be seen from *In Parenthesis* onward and which finally feeds into his later inscriptions.

Despite the broadening of its possibilities with allusion and flexibility of language, *In Parenthesis* follows a conventional narrative arc; this is its macro-structural imperative, the crux of its integration. *In Parenthesis* is a far cry from the non-linear experience of 'reading' form that Jones had experienced in his visual art, and a frustration with that seems evident in the in the description of moving through the 'restricting corridor' of a trench at night in Part 3 of the poem. The inability to see far ahead, to move 'left or right' come to apply as much to the experience of linear narrative as to the trench, while John Ball's 'night phantasm mazes a pre-war, more idiosyncratic skein, weaves with stored-up very other tangled threads' in a way descriptive of a very different narrative experience, that works to

> carry you on dream stuff
> up hill and down again
> show you sights your mother knew,
> show you Jesus Christ lapped in hay with Uncle Eb and his diamond dress-stud next the ox and Sergeant Milford taking his number, juxtapose, dovetail, web up, any number of concepts, and bovine lunar tricks.[48]

As before, there is a primary subject, the tricks of the mind in darkness, but there is once again a subtext, the tricks of the mind in writing. For, take away Sergeant Milford, and Jones has written a prediction of *The Anathémata's* manner and subject matter, already on his mind.

The Anathémata mazes a very idiosyncratic skein indeed; it is not just an ideological poem as discussed, but an idio-logical poem. As Jones expressed it in a letter to Harman Grisewood in 1938, only a year after *In Parenthesis'* publication, *The Anathémata's* structural imperative is based on his hope that,

> if you just talk about a lot of things as one thing follows another, in the end you *may* have made a shape out of all of it. That is to say, that shape that all the mess makes in your mind[49]

The tone of '*may* ' and 'mess' signal his frustration with the demands and limitations of shaping such an idiosyncratic set of ideas into one shape, and the sprawl of *The Anathémata* tends to support that intuition.[50] There is no getting around the fact that language cannot be shaped in quite the same way as purely visual forms and still retain its comprehensibility with ease, certainly not on as large a scale as *The Anathémata* or *In Parenthesis*; on the scale of the inscriptions, however, it may.

They, as Jones says, are 'the connecting link between my drawings and writings',[51] and more importantly, the link between visual abstraction, linguistic abstraction and the bridging activities of *The Anathémata*. 'What says his mabinogi' (fig.1) takes as its main text a small section of *The Anathémata*, with the additional words 'Nadolig bendgaid' (blessed Christmas), and 'Multifarium multisque modis' encircling the whole. In *The Anathémata* the section is set out as below:

What says his *mabinogi*?
        Son of Mair, wife of jobbing carpenter
        in via nascitur
        lapped in hay, *Parvule.*
But what does his Boast say?
                Alpha es et O
                      that which
        the whole world cannot hold.
        Atheling to the heaven-king.
        Shepherd of Greekland.
        Harrower of Annwn.
        Freer of the Waters.
        Chief Physician and
        dux et pontifex.

        Gwledig Nefoedd and
        Walda of *every* land
        et vocabitur WONDERFUL.[52]

The inscription forms the text, at first sight, into a contiguous block, discarding the lineation and italicisings of the printed version: '*Alpha es et o* ', for instance, is no longer dignified by either but by the more subtle placing of the dots between each word, and its expansion alongside the condensed 'that wch' with which it shares a line. Moreover, the inscription is set out as one sentence, to be read continuously. Apart from the spacing marks (the dots as above and the star on the fourth line), the only punctuation marks are two colons that replace the question marks of the text in *The Anathémata*, reinforcing invitation to reading the text continuously. Where question marks and indentation set them apart in the book, in the inscription the colons and arrangement make them linguistically and spatially contiguous with the whole. While 'nadolig bendigaid' on the right of the inscription has a degree of separateness, being a Christmas greeting linked to, but not part of, the text, 'Multifarium multusque modis' replaces the book's '*et vocabitur* WONDERFUL', in a move toward making the audience see the inscription as a whole. As Jones states in a letter to Helen Sutherland, 'Latin has the extra advantage of presenting one with a sort of pattern first' before the meaning becomes apparent', and here the positioning of the words makes it necessary to see them as pattern first, placed as they are, upside-down and then on their side. Even so positioned, the book's English 'WONDERFUL' would be instantly recognisable and detract from the sense of the whole; whereas the Latin allows us to view the words as a yoking line very deliberately drawing together the whole, before we read them. The sense of contiguity then applies itself to the diverse cultural references of the piece: while they yoke the nativity to the military kingship myths of our island via the ancient Welsh deposits of Christianity by forming a single continuous sentence out of references to each, the shape of the whole reinforces the sense that they all belong together as offshoots of one cultural root, rather than merely as fitting terms from heterogeneous sources. Furthermore, the flexibility of hand-lettering as opposed to the rigidity of print, allows the Celtic and Roman letter forms, though recognisably in the same style, to differentiate words in a more subtle way than lineation or italicisation. The shaping of the inscription is at once far more strongly imposed, and more subtle than that of the printed text, and the unity of the whole impresses itself on the reader more so as a result.

The synthesis achieved here and in certain of the other inscriptions (particularly 'Cara Wallia Derilicta', 'Beird Byt Barnant', 'Arbora Decora' and 'Cloelia Cornelia),[53] is a result of Jones forcing the viewer into a new standpoint. The words are chosen, arranged and formed so that we view them first as we would view a painting, before we read them as we would a poem. We are returned to Maritain's distinction between 'intuitively grasped' and 'hieroglyphic' significance: forced to look and intuit before we decipher. As Jones says, 'I expect if one… could read it at a glance, a good bit of the "magic" goes, because one would see the words and their meaning first'.[54] The 'magic' of the painted inscriptions is a welding of the formal abstraction of visual art and the linguistic abstraction of the poetry – a return to Jones' 'first principle' of making, and a vindication of its truth.

Notes:

[1] *Epoch and Artist*, David Jones, ed. Harman Grisewood (London 1973) p.31
The '*implicitly*' is merely drawing attention the previous paragraph's 'explicitly' in relation to *The Anathémata*'s subject matter.

[2] *Epoch* p150

[3] *One Thing At A Time*, Harman Grisewood (London 1968) p.84

[4] See 'Art and Sacrament', *Epoch and Artist* p.175, and below on p.4

[5] *The Dying Gaul and Other Writings*, David Jones, ed. Harman Grisewood (London 1978) p.132

[6] *Dying Gaul* p.134

[7] *Dying Gaul* p.130

[8] *Art in Theory, 1900-2000* ed. Charles Harrison and Paul Wood (Padstow, 2003) p.107

[9] For example, the discussion of *Ars* and *Prudentia* in 'Art and Sacrament' owes a very great deal to Maritain's exploration of the two, with Jones noting that he quotes 'from memory … the translation … made c.1923 by the late Mgr. John O'Connor', while the original analogy between art and war in 'Art in Relation to War', however instinctively sensed by Jones, owes much to Maritain's ' the fine arts … partake, as do the chase or the military art, of the virtues of governance.'.

[10] *Philosophy of Art : being "Art et Scholastique" / by Jacques Maritain*, trans. Rev. John O'Connor (Ditchling, 1923) p.85-6

[11] *Philosophy of Art* p.87

[12] *Philosophy of Art* p.35

[13] *Philosophy of Art* p.117

[14] *The Anathémata*, David Jones (London 1972, first published 1952) p.15

[15] *Epoch* p.175

[16] *Epoch* p.175

[17] *The Shape of Meaning in the Poetry of David Jones*, Thomas Dilworth (Toronto 1988) p.10

[18] *Epoch* p.265

[19] *Epoch* p.265

[20] *Dying Gaul* p.44 The same inverted commas occur when Jones states that Ben Nicholson 'became more and more an apostle of the "abstract"' in a letter of 1936 (*Greatcoat* p.82)

[21] *Epoch* p.98

[22] *Dai Greatcoat – A Self Portrait of David Jones in His Letters* ed. René Hague (London 1980) p.80

[23] *Shape of Meaning* p.52

[24] *Shape of Meaning* p.53

[25] *Shape of Meaning* p.53

[26] *Greatcoat* p.80

[27] *Greatcoat* p.80

[28] *Greatcoat* p.62

[29] Colin Wilcockson, 'David Jones and the Waste-Land Motif', *Inklings 18* (2000) 107 120, p.118

[30] *Philosophy of Art* p.115

[31] *The Sleeping Lord and Other Fragments*, David Jones (London 1974) p.101

[32] *Sleeping Lord* p.101

[33] *In Parenthesis*, David Jones (London 1961, first published 1937) p.ix

[34] *Sleeping Lord* p.107

[35] *Anathémata* p.28

[36] *Anathémata* p.29

[37] *Dying Gaul* p.33

[38] *Sleeping Lord* p.60

[39] See *The Anathémata* pp.15-16, and Wilcockson's 'David Jones and "The Break"', *Agenda* Vol.15 Nos.2-3.

[40] *Dying Gaul* p.17

[41] Jones explores the difference between machine-driven *praxis* fragment and Christian *poiesis* 'A, a, a, Domine Deus', saying

> I have watched the wheels go round in case I might see the living creatures like the appearance of lamps, in case I might see the Living God projected from the Machine. I have said to the perfected steel, be my sister and for the glassy towers I thought I felt some beginnings of His creature, but *A, a, a, Domine Deus*, my hands found the glazed work unrefined and the terrible crystal a stage-paste ... *Eia, Domine Deus*.

[42] *Anathémata* p.50

[43] 'Jesus Christ – they're coming through the floor, endthwart and overlong', *In Parenthesis* p.180

[44] *Anathémata* p.90

[45] *Epoch* p.195

[46] The phrase is also a recognition of the influence of *The Waste Land*, recalling 'These fragments I have shored against my ruins'.

[47] *Anathémata* p.33

[48] *In Parenthesis* p.32

[49] *Greatcoat* p.86

[50] The formal shaping is a separate problem to 'the bloody difficulty of writing about "ideas" and somehow making them concrete', about which Jones is more optimistic, saying 'I believe it can be done.' (*Greatcoat* p.88)

[51] *The Painted Inscriptions of David Jones* ed. Nicolete Gray (London, 1981) p.103

[52] *Anathémata* p.207

[53] Catalogue numbers 49, 47, 39 and 50 respectively. See also Wilcockson's excellent analysis of 49 in 'Mythological References in Two Painted Inscriptions of David Jones', *Journal of Modern Literature* *XXIII, 1* (1999), 173 182

[54] *Inscriptions* p.106

Tony Conran

Everworlds

Second Movement

Benedictus

As Dew in Aprill

The Jesu moves down the
Waters, down the dark
Channels of Miriam, and

As embryo – as every
Embryo – re-enacts
Earth's genesis

When the Holy One
Nosed through the blackness
Of unborn stars

Out from the everworlds
Into the cry
Of a drop of dew.

Conscript

How did these everworlds of sorrow
Ever start? Tides lapping
At the edges

Of our imagining, a salt
Bitterness that never forgets
Or arrives at now?

Through the blitzed streets
Of slums
A private soldier

In battle-dress, but on leave
Whistles tunelessly
In the dawn.

Grey boots echo-sound
Round rubble – this neighbour
Or that's known hearth

Like black flotsam, wood
Singed by the sea.
The soldier pays

No heed. Boots
Chart a course
Through the shoals

Of would-be time, yesterdays
Dirtied by loss.
He is walking home.

His eye reaches for it –
Bitterness that never forgets
Or arrives at now.

The Fossil Collector

Like a Bedouin child, God
Walks in the desert.
A blue-faced Tuareg, a gypsy

Of the dust, he makes for
Where he last found humanity,
Oasis, camping ground

In the sub-zero dune.
Through the foam of the constellations
His lantern steers, into every

Deserted tent
The sharp cry of its light
Prizing out love.

Radio Hams

Who was it said, 'Poets
Don't hunger to be applauded
But believed'?

So do everworld creatures hunger for time,
Even commit murder
To experience a moment, to

Gulp it down, one jab
Of reality, looking out
From frightened eyes

At the Ordinariness – to them
A splendour
Beyond their imagining.

All the technology of dreams
Devotes itself to this:
Inverting their longing

And tainting our souls with it
So that the poison
Enters us like hunger.

The Everworlds crowd round us
Listening as we transmit
Their music back to them:

Hearing the slight distortion,
Wow or pre-echo
Of our dying,

They scrape it off, and chew it
For the faint taste it carries
Of wasted Time.

God in the Everworlds

God came into the Everworlds.
Nobody noticed him.
'Right,' said God,

And he sat down in the green
Room of a wood
To invent himself –

An impressario of the holy
Dancing like the ripple of leaves
His catkins of folly.

The music of miracles
Flowered like yuccas
White spires of lost causes

Bodying to the dawn
His exuberant disasters
Through a narrative of thrushes.

Revelators of his grace
Hoarse as an oracle
Of crouching toads –

The Master of Ceremonies
Flicking comets
Out of his hat …

God standing in the crater of himself
Like a black meteorite
Of denial.

Everworlders were confused.
They'd crept in to see the show,
And here he was

Facing them out, and yet
Not seeing them, the antique
Unconsciousness of a god.

He held them there. At last
One of them clambered
To the mountain of his silence,

Tugged at his sleeve.
'Mr Nijinsky,' she said,
'Will you dance for us?'

God looked at her. 'Dance?' he said,
'What shall I dance?'
She shrank from him.

Ancient greed in her
Glittered like a sea-creature
Brought up in a net.

'Maestro,' she whispered,
'Will you dance Time for us?
Will you dance Time?'

'Time's a long way off,' said God.
'We dream of it,' she said.
'Some of us have seen it.'

God turned from her, a mountain again
In the distance, a grey
Planet. 'Will you dance for us?'

The mountain breathed softly.
'Yes,' said God,
'I will dance you your peace.'

Patricia McCarthy

'How could wounds in that bed of planets – shine, Out-heroding glow-worms?'

Tony Conran: *What Brings You Here So Late?*, Gwasg Carreg Gwalch, 2008, £7.50

There is no doubt that Tony Conran is a poet of considerable stature, insufficiently recognised, certainly outside Wales, and this essay attempts to redress this. He has an impressive and substantial corpus of poetry behind him and is very much part of the modernist tradition, in line with David Jones, Lynette Roberts and Basil Bunting. As such, he is a real *Agenda* poet.

This very recent work of his in the twilight years of his life, a single long autobiographical poem, divided into four symphonic movements, is a major one. It can hold its head high in the company of Basil Bunting's *Briggflatts*, also entitled 'An Autobiography', and conceived of as a sonata as opposed to a symphony, as well as T. S. Eliot's journey into and through himself in *Four Quartets*. Bunting's words in the coda to his long poem, 'A strong song tows us, / long ear-sick' apply beautifully to Conran's work here. Conran's language is as honed and sharp as Bunting's, though more musically varied, it seems to me, in its invention. He does indeed seem to have taken hold of the legacy T. S. Eliot left: to teach poets after him more about music. Thankfully lacking the overt didacticism employed at times by Eliot, Conran's work contains profound philosophy – often existentialist – and theology, even if this is a kind of 'irreligious' theology, as his life transcends the personal and becomes a cosmic quest.

What Brings You Here So Late evokes Conran's childhood in wartime Wales, his student days and his ensuing life as a poet and Catholic in Bangor, coming to terms with his own imminent death when he undergoes spinal surgery to halt his increasing physical paralysis. The many phrases, chants and patterns of images become leitmotifs repeated at different times, reminiscent of T. S. Eliot's repeated images and phrases that evolve into new meanings as they develop in *Four Quartets*. The poem is widely ranging in poetic, filmic, narrative, impressionistic, dramatic, allegorical, even nursery-rhyme and fairy-tale techniques, interwoven with Irish and Welsh mythologies which he makes totally his own, and with biblical references.

In a very early collection, *Formal Poems* (1960), which show Conran to be a consummate formalist with singing lines, Conran invokes 'old names' of Welsh shamans or bards such as Taliesin 'with light in his forelocks,/ That changed before the Huntress / To the very weft of the wind', Gwydion 'diviner and poet – who gave / A girl's lilt to a rose', Tudur, Iolo, Dafydd, and so on. These ancient bards were diviners, visionaries and healers who understood poetry's power to confront and thereby, often in a cathartic form, to remove or transform the suffering or wounding. Conran understands, along with his own primal wound of having been born with cerebral palsy – 'my wired bones / Spastically cursed, my poet's speech / Robbed of an outward intonation' – the wounds of others. One of these is the Welsh poet, R. Williams Parry (died 1955) whose wounds were 'glinting / Like frosty rivers / That we always knew / Ran through our land.' Love is proposed by Conran as the possible cure for wounds where 'the hurt stabs out / No more with vivid / And desperate drums'.

Melanie Reinhart, in her book, *Chiron and the Healing Journey* (1989, Penguin), shows how 'in every shamanic tradition, the candidate must undergo a period of intense psychological, physical and spiritual trial'. He must undertake a journey, even traverse the land of the dead and return in order, as an intermediary, to gain access to the 'realms of the sacred' and become a transformative 'channel for interspecies communication'. Conran does precisely this.

His 'trial' is his cerebral palsy that caused him to be 'a boy built wrong / That had to be hedged with splints, / With excuses', 'a crooked man', 'the warped one' whose voice, even, is 'crumpled', and this is his particular reason for being an outsider. However, in the course of his 'journey', the outsider theme expands into a universal one and Conran could be anyone struggling 'in this country of me', with 'no roots in the world'. Typical of most loners, he often feels consigned to a 'hermitage' which is not necessarily an imprisoning place but a 'visionary' one where 'Patterns in the loneliness / Were etched with light', and from which he 'watched Apollo'. This hermitage opens out when he is gripped by 'A theology of love' and it becomes 'Suddenly / A field full of folk' i.e. the poet is isolated no longer while under love's spell. Elsewhere, for example in the somewhat David Jonesian poem, 'Chapter 13 – The Pit', Conran 'traverses the land of the dead' as part of his shamanic training. He descends down a typical Welsh mine at Abertyssog which becomes an updated classical underworld whose entrance in the valley is 'Blaen Rhymni'. From here the poet, having wandered in and out of commonplace reality, emerges as a shaman or visionary.

In 'Chapter 2 – Unfinished Symphony', (each poem is divided into a chapter similar to a roman-à-clef), 'The *Unfinished* was vision'. The music transforms him and gives him intimations of the sublime or 'sacred'. It is his own self he is listening to, 'Understood / Beyond understanding':

Schubert acknowledging me
And what I must die for.

In 'Chapter 6 – Chemistry' he shows his natural predisposition to be a visionary who gave the Sphinx his 'allegiance' coupled with 'wonder': 'I was Pythagoras, opening / To the order of the spheres'.

His journey which is his 'Way of the Cross', even though 'sometimes the stations of my hands were shut', consists of his 'story' or his 'poetry story' – 'How in the Goddess dark, / I find poems', poems that eventually 'slid into the light'. This dark/ light duality mirrors other dualities such as the potency of his poetry, alongside the 'Impotence at my sleeve / Like a propositioning slut.' His self-conscious

100

awareness of his deformed body that he imagines 'covered with warts' contrasts with the beautiful body of his boyhood friend, Philip: 'A body that had wit in itself / Like a tune, a shape of gracenotes'. The cellos, too, are personified as beautiful bodies that talk to him in words. The recurrent image of the 'twin' emphasises duality also. There are 'the twin gates of sleep'. One of his twins is the muse waiting to be born at his first poem who seeks *green words / And a strange locality / To dye / My unborn whiteness // With the leaf / And pastoral homesteads / Of a name*. His 'far-away potency' even enters 'like a twin' into the flesh of Liz, his girlfriend; the creation of a poem is likened to the sex act – '*the poet is the male spirit*' creating, ultimately, '*the new child*.'

Between the two polarities of birth when the poet was 'hatched' by the world, and death, the reader follows Conran's 'story' or journey through his growth to maturity, via the 'immortals', 'eternals' and through his own versions of 'theology' interspersed with 'tiny collects of joy'. Indeed it is this 'surging joy' – sometimes sensuous, sometimes abstract – 'as in the giving of pebbles to Dwynwen / where asplenium marinum grows in rock faces // of her island' that Conran counterbalances with pain. In his sparse, exact, yet frequently experimental style, drawing from science, music, his wide reading of the classics and Anglo-Saxon, and of the mystics, he explains his loves, his response to Hiroshima, travel, politics in the Thatcher years about which he gives vent to trenchant satire, personifying materialism, or, as he says, 'wealth in monopoly capitalism', as 'the hag Money', 'Ma Money' 'weeded our hearts. / It was like Dachau, Buchenwald' – and his coming to terms with death in the final two movements. He envisages death, including living deaths, as 'A hooded procession of poisoners / On the high moors'.

Like a dadaist, he sees the absurd which emanates from tragedy as the only way of handling bereavement - as he ruminates on the deaths of each of his three brothers in turn. 'Like Sex, his sister, Brother Death / Is his own man among the platitudes'. He continues in the same tone regarding his own future death, his 'hilarity', a weird 'toddler' that wants to be carried, and whom he has 'run' with 'in the three-legged race'. He shows exemplary spirited resignation to and acceptance of 'little' death that he will carry, like a nursery rhyme, 'A long way yet along my crooked mile'.

Conran mythologises his own life very effectively, revealing the complex levels and layers in the psyche. He uses alter egos like archetypal figures from a fairytale, such as the Leopard for his conventional childish self, the reiterated name 'poor love', who 'walked with Dante by the Menai', both to explain, and to objectify and depersonalise his physically crippled self. In the final symphonic movement, he becomes the childish 'platypus' and defiant 'warrior'. Together with the preponderance of allegorical figures in this sequence, Conran's alter egos serve to illustrate the way he deals with his wound. His weaving of them in and out of the four movements emphasises the need to externalise the self. He hints also that perhaps in our journeys through life, we never properly grow up, or are indeed 'frightened to grow up', remaining children, and even anonymous, particularly in the face of death, when viewed in the visionary light of the shaman. The toy images, and nursery-rhyme patter such as 'wee, wee, wee', '"Ho", said my father', the 'Ho, Catulllus' cried by the leopard and later 'Ho, Jesu', that recur intermittently throughout the sequence, succinctly reinforce this.

The extremely moving 'Finale' (the fourth movement) containing a lot of dramatic dialogue brings to a climax many images already stated. Stressed again is the wounding, his worsening cerebral palsy. An operation is imminent to avoid paralysis; the theme of physical beauty evidenced at the beginning in the shape of his youthful friend, Philip, recurs in the form of the surgeon who will operate on him and who appears in a variety of guises. On the larger foreground of the world's stage in a Beckettian 'no-man's-land', the surgeon, an equally nameless 'solitary man,' is 'handsome, with cropped curls / Of yellow hair'. His clothes: a green linen cloak and white shirt hark back to the unborn muse awaiting creation at Conran's first poem in the first movement. She names these very colours – 'green words' to dye 'her unborn whiteness'. This way, Conran cleverly gives his long poem a circular shape.

The surgeon is also a 'friendly god / One of the Immortals' who links to other immortals in previous movements. He then becomes the named Lugh from the Táin, the poet's mentor/father figure, a mythological ancient symbol 'from the dancing world / Under the tumulus at Lerga' who disappears to the mundane 'clatter of wheelchairs' and contrasts with Conran's real mainly unsympathetic father at the beginning of this work. The theme of sleep, a sleep that must be trusted, or one that can kill recalls the sleep theme elsewhere and leads to the choice that the surgeon offers the poet – like the choice faced by Arthurian knights when they went in search of the Holy Grail – upon which the poet constructs a rhyme or jingle to deal with the serious job the surgeon has to perform – to save his 'neck from the high gallows tree'.

Despite the taunting and jeering song about his increasing disability croaked by the sinister Morrigu, also drawn from The Táin, Thomas Kinsella's translation of the Dark Age Irish epic saga, *Táin bo Cuailnge,* the poet insists that he can still see, still work and gather 'assemblies / Of woven words'. The use of both the Morrigu and Lugh broaden the perspective and scope of the sequence and universalise it further. As at the beginning of the book, the poet is never self-pitying. He has endured his disability with humility and acceptance, and has created a far-reaching, enlightening world and body of poetry out of it, despite his wading 'like an animal / Bent with wounds', despite the Morrigu watching him 'like carrion / On the red gravel'.

The last poems, situated in hospital, in intensive care and on the ward, illustrate the shadowy, half conscious, distorted post-operative world of the patient. Body parts and medical terminology prevail but the perspective is that of the poet who now calls himself 'platypus' because the oxygen-mask felt like a duck's bill. Time, with its 'contorted voices' is askew and belongs more to an ancient megalithic era with its chambers and tombs; classical allusions are still there with Charon, the boatman, waiting to 'ferry' not the poet but the 'ghost' visitors 'to grief'. Platypus himself sees all his surroundings, whether real or imagined, as shrunken: the soldiers are toy soldiers, there is a toy tomb; he himself feels he is back, as at the beginning of the sequence, in a womb. He is in a place with 'no name', again a bleak Beckettian existentialist world. The surgeon becomes an 'otherworld Orpheo', but the 'empty grave' in the final line is no glib happy-ever-after note of survival. Normal chat and normal perspectives resume and Conran is just about managing again to take up survival's tune.

The over-riding image towards the end of the four symphonic movements is that of the dance. Earlier, his poems had 'danced' for a girl but now, saved by Lugh who comes from 'the dancing world', it seems that he will, in his 'waltz of bones', not have to join 'The ghostly harvest / Of bones / That danced / Like ripe wheat'. Instead, as a poet/shaman with the power to become the god he dances, he will be able to be that 'impeccable warrior', the wounded-healer, who, as he told the Morrigu in self-defence, 'All his life dances', perhaps, into that 'still point in the turning circle' as outlined by Eliot in *Four Quartets*. From here, Conran might well still write many a 'choreography for voices' as he called one of his early works, dancing his words along their lines.

It could be proposed that wounds 'out-heroding glow-worms' lie behind the most enduring poetry. When Yeats, another of Conran's mentors, appears as a ghost during Conran's visit to Ben Bulben, Conran is moved to tears. The engine, or driving-force, behind nearly all of Yeats' finest poems was basically the lasting wound of his unrequited love for Maud Gonne, and the writing of the poetry itself performed a kind of healing. Indeeed without any wounding, Yeats and Conran might have resorted to what Yeats suggested had he gained Maud Gonne's undying love: 'I might have thrown poor words away / and been content to live'. Such a loss this would have been.

By the end of his symphony, it is apparent that Conran has gained access to 'the realms of the sacred' and to 'vision' – as he set out to do in a very early poem:

> Even the blind, the very lame, are free
> Can they but conform to the strict dance
> That to the outward eye is but form,
> Hypnosis of the jerking ghost, yet
> Secretly is consecration – giving
> And taking to an eternal tune.

May he flourish, therefore, consecrated, but not 'secretly', in his 'eternal tune'.

Johnny Marsh

Painting, Poetry, Music: The Images of Pascale Petit

In these two collections of poetry, *The Treekeeper's Tale* (Seren, 2008) and an imminent collection, *What the Water Gave Me*, Pascale Petit curates her images with a painter's eye. Paintings are at the core of the poems, those of Frida Kahlo, Remedios Varo and Franz Marc, also her own works. The image is the starting point in creating works where the distinctions of the arts are blurred, producing a liminal zone at the meeting of poetry, painting and music.

In *The Treekeeper's Tale* it is the violence towards the earth that is invoked by the images, especially in the first and the third sections. She describes the Redwood forests of California

> Where we see ourselves as part of the forest,
> the thought emerging
> like a white doe who keeps a shy distance,
> at home in the heart of the grove.

Her vision of Europe devastated by the First World War, evoked through the paintings of Franz Marc, focuses on archetypal horses moving amongst the wastes:

>   ...in one
> bound, they'll reach the edge of the trenches,
> where a red mare is giving birth
> to a white colt with wings soft as drifts.

Reminiscent of the mythologies of David Jones's *In Parenthesis* and of Marc Chagall's paintings, the spirit of the horse flies above the land, and through it. Its most recent incarnation may well be in Mark Wallinger's Kentish Horse among the pylons.

The final poems of each of these sections, 'Creation of Trees' and 'The Trees Show their Rings' create a synthesis of music, painting and verse, the act of creation having no boundaries:

> I longed for harmonies to grow the trees,
> so the songs of their light would flood my studio.

And

> The trees unwound their rings
> for dressings to staunch the deepest wounds.

This staunching of wounds ushers in another set of linked images that recur throughout both collections but find a voice in that of Frida Kahlo in *What the Water Gave Me*, and in the second section of *The Treekeeper's Tale*: 'Afterlives'. These are images of violence towards the person, the violence of birth, of childhood, of death – poems/images become objects displayed before us as relics, as archaeology, as precious remnants, the ex voto offering.

> ...Now
> I am displayed in this museum, my clothes
> and sacred ornaments on mannequins behind glass,
> my body naked.

She displays things upon which violence has been done – and shows how these wounds are repaired, or held by tree rings, vines, roots, veins, sinews and thread – bindings through which nourishment and pain flow.

'Mexico grew out of its wounds', says Carlos Fuentes in his introduction to the Diary of Frida Kahlo. Pascale Petit's poems in *What the Water Gave Me* have grown from the wounds of Frida Kahlo who articulates and gives voice to her pain through paint. Throughout this sequence, the image of birth is the first act of violence. This Kleinian reprise is repeated five times in the title poems, and is echoed in the second section, 'Afterlives' of *The Treekeeper's Tale* where birth and death, and death in birth are entwined, enlaced and embroidered together by means of

> each dancing thread and singing stitch.

It is said by Kahlo's biographer, Hayden Herrera, that Frida 'took to her clothes as a nun to the veil'. Appearing always in theatrical indigenous attire, costumes bedecked with jewels, she linked herself with her pre-Columbian origins, in anticipation of a living shroud, preparing for 'an enormous and very silent exit'. Her life was a life of performance. This exotic exoskeleton focuses attention upon the broken body beneath, held together by threads and sinews. Indeed, images of sewing and needles weave their way through the poems, illuminating

> A gash sewn with sinews.

The traditionally feminine arts of the needle, the reparations of sewing, contrast with the violence of the medical needle, intrusive and penetrative, masculine: the needle wielded to empower or to control.

Throughout *What the Water Gave Me*, there is a tension between empowerment and dependency. These are Frida's themes and also the themes underlying the corpus of Pascale Petit's poetry. The poetry is strongest where the image is the focus. The constant recurrence of gynaecological and anatomical detail in *What the Water Gave Me* can become repetitive and too much of an affect. Although it is an integral part of the experience, it perhaps could have been used more sparingly.

The poems' success lies in the detail, in the images of fruit, flowers, animals and birds that are the 'forest murmurs' throughout, and the leitmotivs that stitch her life and art together as she creates her personal mythology.

This as yet unpublished sequence belongs to an expanding area of poetic works, that of the connection between poetry and painting through exhibitions. Fourteen of these poems were originally published as *The Wounded Deer – Fourteen Poems after Frida Kahlo*, to coincide with the Frida Kahlo exhibition at the Tate Modern in 2005. The biographical sequence/response is an integral part of the curation and commissioning of exhibitions. Similar projects have been inspired by other painters and sculptors from Bonnard to Cornell; also recently in Ruth Padel's collection about her great, great grandfather, Charles Darwin: *Darwin: A Life in Poems*. The life, or the works, themselves a sequence, becomes a score upon which the poet can orchestrate, embellish, explain, and question the works and their position towards them.

Personally I find this a welcome addition to the critical commentaries that accompany exhibitions. It is like finding familiar, or not so familiar texts that have been annotated by a different hand in which one has a faith. There is a sincerity in these footnotes and in their form as a sequence. It becomes a journey, a mirroring of the experience of looking around exhibitions, or around the span of a life, or a body of work. As in music, this adds duration and direction.

Pascale Petit

Translating Yang Lian's 'The Valley and the End: A Story'

'You close the book then close the riverbanks'

The history of Chinese poetry is rooted in the Chinese landscape. This is why we've come to the legendary Yellow Mountain to translate each other's poems, a whole group of us, including W. N. Herbert, Robert Minhinnick, Wang Xiaoni, Yang Lian and myself. This is where the Yellow Emperor sought the elixir of immortality from an islet in one of the misty 'seas' that form in the valleys between peaks.

To the 'deep-reality' poet Yang Lian, the Tang Dynasty tradition cannot be ignored. His images are loaded with it. It's as if Yellow Mountain, this mist-enshrouded idyll so familiar from scroll paintings, lies as a wash on each blank page as he starts to write. And from each page, fog swirls to form ghost-valleys, rivers of exile. Peaks rise with names such as Bookcase Peak and Writing Brush Bursts into Bloom. In the 'seas', images flower then fade. The fog is thick as cocoon silk – opaque enough to hold memories of London in its weave. On a bank of cumulus Walthamstow Marshes floats. I glimpse dragon-boats, an iron bridge, a marina café where a couple confront one another. No sooner do they appear than their faces melt like sugar lumps in tea. There are photos on the wall, faded sepia shots. Outside, a swan slices the water and it starts to rain. The café vapourises with a furnace-hiss.

The long raindrops are chopsticks stabbing the surface, breaking it up. A bath floats between the fish-rings. The woman's six-year-old self lies inside the white enamel, and as the sun sets, its rays tint her bathwater red. A flock of birds are nailed to the sky by the clock's hour hand, which in Mandarin is a needle not a hand.

So while I wait on the mountain steps, wedged in the crowd, I mull over how to make this image work in English. There's plenty of time. The queue waiting to climb Celestial Peak is packed with Chinese tourists. My task is to render the original poem as naturalistically as possible, as if it had originally been written in English, yet preserve those images, now stone, now mist, that merge into one another. A small white moth lands on the twisted lower branch of Welcoming Guests Pine. He has a tiny black-and-gold striped mountain range painted across his wings, and as I wait for the queue to move, he soars back up to the sky, taking his miniature Huangshan with him.

And now I've climbed the crag of the highest peak, and it's time to descend the too-narrow stone steps carved into black rock with buff stripes, this sky-tiger I'm riding through the haze, and I have to concentrate on each step so as not to fall off the unfenced razor drop on my right. I chant the names to myself to fight off vertigo – Lotus Pistil Peak, Cloud-Dispelling Pavilion, Echo Wall. I reach the rock where a monk once drew the character for lightning and made it crack, and I have to pass right through this slit towards Jade Screen Peak. At times the striated rock sways like the banks of comfrey and chamomile I've squeezed through on the Marshes, the scent of meadowsweet making me giddy. Over the Carp's Backbone to the Gold Cock Crowing at Heaven's Gate and I'm pushing harder now as it's getting late and the telpher shuts at dusk. The mountain will close and press me flat as a flower in a book.

Flat as Walthamstow Marshes, my neck of the woods, now Lian's locale, only he lives on the Hackney side and I in Walthamstow. We might as well be on Yellow Mountain in this desolate poem where mouths hang from walls, where light flashes off the river Lee like a tiger's pelt, one stripe in London, one in China.

Imagine my surprise as he sits in my tiny study, the mournful cries of geese crossing the window's sky, while he conjures the marshes in faltering Yanglish, and I search the clouds for the right words to translate his lines. Geese, which have flown over my house all these years, suddenly are the wild geese of exile, their calls evoking homesickness as potently as they did in the time of Li Bai writing poems on Celestial Peak.

I've lived in North East London for over twenty years now and would have moved away long ago except for that nearby sanctuary, with its head-high wildflowers and the Springfield Marina where 'The Valley and the End: A Story' takes place. I've often stopped at the small riverside café for a cup of tea and a cake to warm me during walks. Last time I passed it was closed, which was a shame because I wanted to check out those old photos in his poem.

Lian's images are collages of strangely juxtaposed objects, but he considers his surrealism to be 'deep reality' – imagery with roots, rather than a surrealism that might just be obscure or playful ornament. As a former sculptor I am interested in image-making in my own poems. The pictorial aspect of the Chinese characters fascinates me. Yang Lian's poetry is a new kind of image-making for British poetry, which tends to stick to straightforward narrative. He isn't just conjuring the world but remaking it into a system of concentric symbols, an organic collage of deep reality. I question him about every phrase, its sound and sense, until it starts to root in my imagination and re-grow.

In his essay 'A Wild Goose Speaks To Me' (*Poetry Review*, Spring 2006) he wrote: 'Give me a single breath, and I will grow roots, penetrate the soil, probe shingle and magma, and hear the sea through every artery and vein of groundwater'. He went on to say, '"local" doesn't at all signify a specific site, but must point to all sites, as being the ability of the poet to excavate his own self'.

In writing his new collection *Lee Valley Poems* (Bloodaxe, 2009), Yang Lian makes Lee Valley's waters turn twelve hundred years upstream to their source, which for him is the Tang Dynasty. The further they flow, the nearer he accesses his innermost self. This poem 'The Valley and the End: A Story' occurs in a non-time implied by the tenselessness of the Chinese verb, which is a challenge to translate into English. That couple waiting for the end are always on the marshes, sitting in the café, which is simultaneously a Huangshan path. To

Lian's eyes, the café walls are banded Mesozoic rock where Li Bai and Du Fu's shadows pass, each drunk on their own solitudes. But however heavy the theme and weighted the history, the lines must fly. Like that Huangshan moth bearing a mountain on its wings.

Yang Lian

The Valley and the End: A Story

i

The days blend into each other – we keep saying the same old things.
The sky is a raincoat with a dripping hem.
Rain taps on white tables in old photos
and on two cups of half-drunk tea. All afternoon we counted the upturned chairs.
Our mouths have hung from the wall for fifty years.

ii

Everywhere is ending. When you stop reading,
light leaps from the water's pelt. When you pull back your hand,
no longer touching the beast's gorgeous stripes,
your name is the same but sealed off by the weather,
like that loud green on the far bank gradually departing.

iii

A pear tree blocks the balcony
and its spring bedroom full of naked flowers.
On the grass, birds hatch opalescent light.
Our bodies accept the coldness of a past life
by the way they touch and this still makes you wet.

iv

A sugar lump melts an old woman's squeaking bones –
we can watch her machinery, drop by drop,
leaking tea, swathing her groans
in vapour. Time begins at the next table,
passes the sweetness of the end through our guts.

v

Fish-rings wait for us outside the window.
We walked over that pale gravel path
to where a million fish eye-socket circles
are pierced by chopsticks of rain – the circles' centres
choked by the softest diameter.

vi

You close the book then close the riverbanks.
Swan-stares carve this view –
the house, the iron bridge, that silently emerge –
their paddling feet are russet leaves under the water's surface
where our presence secretly shatters a cloud.

vii

Dive back into the six-year-old's bathtub.
Just six years old, the body, already smashed open
by a blood-red torrent, has become a dirty word,
the air made even thinner the further back time reels.
What dives back into the girl's eyes is raw poetry

viii

but it's not love poetry. Why waste time
by talking about time? We are the valley's delicacies.
We listen to the weightless horseshoe of the crescent moon
splashing mud on our faces – so cold a reunion
forces us to sink even deeper.

ix

History gradually darkens, replicating our organs.
An old filament secretes a film of twilight.
That gas ring pierces thin fingers,
the flames spurt, hissing five o'clock with a furnace roar –
the entire sky of homing birds, each one nailed to the clock's hour hand.

x

Two ends – either yes or no.
Two ends like two people face to face, holding up the same cup
to keep warm – a present tense you spill from your clothes.
Two memories glide between stars at the speed of light,
a black umbrella lifted by a disembodied hand orbits

xi

all sorrow and joy – just to be alive.
While we sit at the table against the blankness of water,
water flows away unnoticed.
The end is never like the sea, rain snuffs out one second
then we forget our past.

xii

Naked sex converges on one point in the sky,
licks the emerald breasts of wild ducks.
Trees in fog are truly beautiful. That old photo
bathed in moonlight is the park inviting you for a stroll.
The night sky is so close, hiding at your back, inviting you to moan fiercely.

Translated from the Chinese by **Pascale Petit**

Cary Archard

The Power of Translation: the influence of Rilke
on Alun Lewis and Dannie Abse

Rilke, that most single-minded and European of poets, was born in Prague, attended school in Vienna, studied at the universities of Prague, Munich and Berlin, lived in many different places across Europe, before dying at the age of fifty-one in 1926 in Switzerland. He wrote in German but nevertheless became an enormously influential figure for a number of important Anglophone poets who were at responsive stages of their careers in the late 1930s and early 40s. Translations into English began to appear in the early Thirties (from the Hogarth press, for example) and as that decade darkened, so Rilke's influence grew. He was seen as a model of how a poet should live and the language and imagery of his poems resonated in the minds of young writers caught up in the Depression and the Second World War.

It is hard to over-state Rilke's appeal. Visiting America in 1940, and casting about for a comparison to describe night on the Hudson River, MacNeice wrote: 'It was something such as Rilke meant by Death, something unknown but comprehensive where everything falls into place'.[1] Staying in North Carolina, at the start of September that same year, Elizabeth Bishop wrote in a letter that she was 'reading Rilke's Wartime Letters, which I think are terrifying, but full of wonderful things'[2]. It wasn't just his darkness that attracted these poets. They found, in Rilke, images and strategies for confronting the unknown and unfamiliar in their own lives. Auden, whose writing began to show signs of Rilke's influence from 1936, following his visit to China two years later, made Sonnet XXIII of his Sonnets to China (they appeared in 'Journey to a War' in March, 1939) his particular tribute to Rilke, who was clearly the presiding model for these poems:

> let me think of one
>
> Who for ten years of drought and silence waited,
> Until in Muzot all his being spoke,
> And everything was given once for all.
>
> Awed, grateful, tired, content to die, completed,
> He went out in the winter night to stroke
> That tower as one pets an animal.[3]

There is a striking similarity between Auden's and MacNeice's views of Rilke. He is portrayed as mystical and messianic: 'something unknown'/ 'one who for ten years of drought and silence waited'; 'everything falls into place'/ 'everything was given once for all'. For these poets, Rilke seems to have some of the qualities more often associated with a religious leader. Bishop is also seduced by the wonder and terror of his writing.

Rilke's power to elicit such interest and devotion is also evident in the lives of the two finest poets of the Second World War. Both of them carried Rilke's poems with them, kept him close, so to speak, while far away from home. Keith Douglas, who served in North Africa during 1941-3 and who was wounded at Wadi Zem Zem, in August 1943 'had with him at Homs a volume of Rilke's *Selected Poems* in a translation by Ruth Speirs, published in Cairo'[4]. The South Walian poet, Alun Lewis also carried with him a volume of Rilke's *Selected Poems* while in India with the South Wales Borderers in 1943. Rilke was so important to him that he lent his copy to Freda Ackroyd, the woman with whom he fell in love while away from his battalion convalescing. Already, on the sea voyage to India, Rilke had entered Lewis's rich dream world. He wrote in his journal: 'He [Rilke] approached me when we were lying off India and I asked him about silence, and what price one paid for going my way – through the panzer divisions of the century – and whether he would have found his silence there'[5]. When Lewis put together his second volume of poems, *Ha! Ha! Among the Trumpets* (1945), he placed the poem 'To Rilke', a poem which builds on his dream and which imagines what Rilke might say if he spoke to him, at the head of the book's third and final section, 'India'. The words he gives to Rilke seem to exclude Lewis himself, for Rilke speaks of 'the devoted' and of 'Humanity's…darlings' and Lewis was not sure that he was one of these. When he describes India in the poem, it is a place of 'darkness' where 'jackals howl and whimper in the nullah'. When Lewis thinks of his wider situation, the war, he writes of 'the self-assertion/ These fierce competing times insist upon'. Comparing himself with the other poet, Lewis envies Rilke's 'silence' and his certainty. The final verse of the poem remembers how sure he had been of his own love for his wife, Gweno, but this is now in 'Oh a distant land'. For Lewis, Rilke acts as a reminder of what poetry means to him. Rilke's silence reminds him of the space which he, too, needs as a way of standing apart from the dangerous situation in which he finds himself. Lewis might have been thinking of Letter Four in Rilke's *Letters to a Young Poet*: 'But your solitude will be a home and a hold for you even amid very unfamiliar conditions and from there you will find all your ways.' His poem is an anxious cry to Rilke to help him in this different world: 'this poem has long been with me, the poem to Rilke. On board ship, sick, waiting for the horizon to disclose the unknown India: now in my tent in the heart of the unknown, India.' It seems extraordinary that a poet Lewis could read only in translation should so haunt him, should speak to him so directly and personally, in these months before his death in Burma the following year.

Rilke played a key part in the development of another poet from Wales in the early Forties. While the soldier poets, Douglas and Lewis, were reading Rilke abroad, at war in 1943, Dannie Abse, who at nineteen had left Cardiff to continue studying medicine in London, moved to Swiss Cottage where he lived among refugees many of whom were Jews from Austria and Germany. It was one of these, Rudi Nassauer, himself a poet, who introduced him to Rilke in translation.

For some years afterwards, he found Rilke's influence inescapable; he 'became a passion for me…Rilke's influence endured and could set me ticking like a wheel of a bicycle'[6]. Abse was impressed by Rilke's extraordinary commitment and the poet quickly became his model:

'This before all: ask yourself in the quietest hour of your night: *must* I write? Dig down into yourself for a deep answer. And if this should be in the affirmative, if you may meet this solemn question with a strong and simple, *I must*, then build your life according to this necessity.' I responded, of course, with a strenuous, 'I must', and I have, though it may sound somewhat grand to say so, unconsciously as much as consciously, ordered my life ever since to allow for this central need.[7]

But Rilke also made the young doctor, with his Jewish, socialist upbringing, very uneasy. In Rilke's self-absorption, his belief that the poet needs isolation and in his tendency to look inwards instead of outwards, he recognised some of his own traits. In his 1948 notebook[8], Abse started work on a poem, that went through many drafts, which was called first, simply, 'Rilke' but which then became 'Rilke the man'. Eventually, many of the lines of this uncompleted poem were used in a poem that was published with the title, 'The Odour of Nothing', which appeared in Abse's second book, *Walking under Water (1952)*. Though the 'you' in the published poem is generalised and avoids specific personal associations, the notebooks show how the Rilke poem became a poem about Abse himself, (as the drafts developed, the title in the notebook changed to 'Argument with Myself'), about the kind of person and kind of poet he should become. In the notebook, the argument with Rilke is clearly stated:

I see my own faults in him, and so would forsake
my silent tryst with the appointed agonies,
even, yes, the gentle exultation of daffodils in the mind
and now would gather them as flowers not as yellow images.

In the published poem, 'The Odour of Nothing', this becomes:

Could you accept existence then, like some animal,
Without question – all that has leaned over you or alighted
Upon you – to kiss for the sake of the kiss
To forsake your silent tryst with the appointed agonies
Even yes, with the alien life of daffodils – to gather them
Only as flowers, not as yellow images?

Having put himself in the place of Rilke, Abse rejects Rilke's emphasis, as he sees it, on 'existence', abstractions, in favour of objects, the world grasped through the senses – 'the dance at five entrances'. In the notebook poem, he spells this out:

Rilke, the man that is, forgot to live, only saying 'I exist':
Standing outside the window, watching the road curves touch each other,
His own experience reinterpreted into Dolls and Angels,
Instead of becoming and being for their own sake.

So for Abse, Rilke played an essential part in his own trajectory as a poet. The youthful Welsh poet's absorption with his own inner life, its pains and pleasures, was damaging his poetry. The poem links Rilke to 'loneliness' and 'solitude', to the role of 'fugitive' and 'voyager' which are seen as destructive pursuits. Abse's argument with Rilke turned him towards experience, and towards the practice of waiting for poems to come to him. Previously his poetry had been a habit 'all played on a harp of nerves'. Rilke helped him see the futility of this. 'The Odour of Nothing' represents a turning point in Abse's direction as a poet. The search for meaning beyond the senses, turning experience in to symbols ('Dolls and Angels') is rejected as it leads to 'the odour of nothing'. The poet posing as a tormented soul, constantly searching for something beyond himself, is also rejected. Throughout the poem, there is an awareness of the ephemeral, an awareness that death is never far away: 'Even now in the Churchyard they are digging a deep hole.' This context heightens the poet's sense of the visible world. His argument with Rilke marks a change in Abse's view of the poet, and a change in his own poetic credo, and eventually in his own style. The published poem concludes:

To become man, human – not merely poet…
Have you accepted this? To go out, to go on,
For reason of the going only, without a destination?

There are hints in the poem that it is the past which will provide a rich vein of subject matter in the future, specifically in the lines: 'For ghosts like portraits/can see you where you look. And the more you go away/ the more they stay.' When he came to look back on this period, Abse said the lesson he should have learnt from Rilke was to focus on experience. But this 1948 poem which, like most of the poems from Abse's first two books, does not appear in his *Collected Poems*, suggests that he had already begun to learn that lesson early on in his relationship with the German poet. Perhaps the influence was working on a deeper level also. In Letter One of *Letters to a Young Poet*, Rilke writes about the past, and childhood in particular, in a way which anyone familiar with Abse's own work would recognise – though it is in his prose works that Abse most frequently writes about his early life. Rilke writes:

And even if you were in some prison the walls of which let none of the sounds of the world come to your senses – would you not then still have your childhood, that precious, kingly possession, that treasure-house of memories?

'The Uninvited', the only poem from his first book, *After Every Green Thing* (1948), that Abse has included in his *Collected Poems,* was stimulated, Abse says, by his reading of the eighth letter in Rilke's *Letters to a Young Poet.* "Rilke, in that letter, spoke of how certain sorrowful experiences alter us because of what they may engender. When we are open to important moments of sorrow, argued Rilke, then our future 'sets foot in us'. Though we could easily believe nothing has truly happened, our destiny begins and 'we have changed as a house is changed into which a guest has entered'." But the poem fits, too, Abse's recognition of the importance of turning away from oneself, from too much emphasis on the inner life and turning instead to the unexpected, the visitation from outside. The rewards which follow can be huge but also frightening:

> They came into our lives unasked for.
> There was light momentarily, a flicker of wings,
> a dance, a voice, and then they went out
> again, like a light, leaving us not so much
> in darkness, but in a different place
> and alone as never before.

The 'wings', the 'voice' and the 'dance', suggestions of the mystical, come from Rilke but the recognition of the power of the outside world to change us comes from Abse's struggle with his mentor's 'inescapable' voice. It is also surely an acknowledgement of the importance of Rilke's 'uninvited' expedition into Dannie Abse's own poetic life.

Notes:

[1] MacNeice, *The Strings are False*, p35, London 2007

[2] Bishop, *The One Art - The Selected Letters*, ed. R Giroux p92, London 1994

[3] Auden, *Collected Poems*, ed. E Mendelson, London 2007

[4] *Keith Douglas*, Desmond Graham, Oxford 1974

[5] Lewis Journals, Bridgend 2009

[6] Abse, *Under The Influence of...*, Cardiff 1984

[7] op cit

[8] Abse, Notebooks, National Library of Wales

Dannie Abse

After the Memorial

Some spoke of her unostentatious beauty:
she, passionate moralist, Truth's sweet secretary.
No-one heard the sobbing of the angels.

Well, I have my own weeping to do.
(If angels could weep they would become human.)
I lived her life and she lived mine –
not only in the easy valleys of Pretend
where bosky paths descend to lakes where no swan
is singular (and fish ignore the hunched Angler)

but here where the uphill road to happiness
has ordinary speed limits,
and still the revelation is
that there can be such a thing

until it must yield to a dead end.

So now our marriage book is drowned
(there seemed magic in it)
and she is both manifest and concealed –
manifest because I see her everywhere,
concealed because she is nowhere to be found.

The Revisit

This scene too beautiful, it seemed a fake:
the unlikely sky, the drowning sunset lake.
With you by my side, did I dream awake?

God's spacious canvases always amaze
even when lucid colours become uncertain greys.
There was nothing else we could do but praise.

Yet darkness, like dread, lay within the scene
and you said, 'Just like music that seems serene.'
(Mozart stared at green till he became the green.)

And there, above the lake, of course unsigned,
its surface hoofed with colour by the wind,
were great windows between clouds, fires behind,

as if from Angel wars. Such April bloodshed!
The wide sky-fires flared and their glitter-red
sparks cooled to scattered stars instead.

Now I, bereaved, like the bruised sky in disrepair,
a shadow by my side, hear a far owl's thin despair.
I stare at colour till I am the stare.

The gradual distance between two stars is night.
Ago, love, we made love till dark was bright.
Now without you dark is darker still and infinite.

Peter Dale

'The old temptation to remould the World'

Alun Lewis: *Collected Poems*, edited by Cary Archard, Seren, £9.99, 206pp.

It has taken a long time for the reconsideration of Alun Lewis, begun by Ian Hamilton in *Selected Poems and Prose* back in 1966, to re-establish him alongside Keith Douglas as one of the two most interesting and promising young poets lost in the Second World War. Lewis's *Collected Poems*, even so, was a long time in coming. Full coverage is still to come.

This *Collected* contains the books Lewis prepared for publication, twenty-seven poems, variously published elsewhere, and a short introduction by the editor, giving details concerning the uncollected poems. It is a reader's rather than a scholarly edition and has no textual or other notes.

Lewis was brought up in Wales in the harsh period before and after the depression. His parents were both teachers; he taught for a time and married Gweno, a teacher of German. He was clearly in what might be termed the ameliorist strand of thought and conduct, as shown by his socialist and pacifistic political activity at college. Later, in the army, he threw himself with enthusiasm into arranging educative lecture courses for the soldiers in camp and entertainments on the troopship. In 'The Jungle', his last poem, he remarks:

And time is swept with a great turbulence,
The old temptation to remould the world.

His well-known poems 'All Day it has Rained', 'To Edward Thomas', 'The Public Gardens', 'To Rilke' and the poems written in India have probably helped to blur his inescapable Welshness as revealed in many other poems. He could never forget the deprivation and the working-class servitude imposed by industrialisation, particularly mining, and the hardships of agricultural life. All of this was exacerbated by the economic depression which affected most of his early life. Nor could he forget that Welsh sense of community and solidarity against the odds and that community of culture in poetry, song and sport. Another aspect of his Welsh ties was his self-defence from all this hardship by taking to the romantic ancient hills and the beautiful coast as a sort of abiding comfort. The third strand in his make-up was an overwhelming need for love and strong personal commitment, a powerful sense of responsibility. These strands weave in and out of his vocation to write, complicating and twisting it for he also had to face that debilitating condition of cash-strapped artists: how to buy time to write without damage to all those commitments. All of these issues were compounded and made more pressing by the coming of war.

Psychologically his personality moved between an energetic impulsiveness and a depressed passiveness. The first is shown, for example, in his wandering off and joining the Engineers apparently merely because he met a recruiting sergeant while he was actually in London to discuss going into the navy. (Lewis, rather like Owen, was almost a conscientious objector – one with a seared conscience. He may have felt that most of the engineers would not have to kill people directly.) The second tendency becomes plain in the Indian poems, such as 'The Mahratta Ghats', which move between his alternating bafflement at the passivity of Indian peasants under their oppression and deprivation and his attraction to their apparent fatalism and acceptance that his near-mystic experiences of Vishnu and the poem 'To Rilke' indicate.

All of these strands variously thread back to the influence of Edward Thomas from whom his poetics were productively developed. Thomas's complex attitude to the First World War along with his depressive and suicidal tendencies also chimed with something in Lewis, suggesting parallels in their situations.

As poet, Douglas was amazingly precocious but Lewis developed much more slowly. In the December after the declaration of war in 1939, Lewis remarked, 'I need at least ten years to work out my spirit in writing.' He was not given those years, consequently his work is uneven.

Douglas was the more extrovert writer, observing both himself and others with an objective and ironic eye. He derives most directly from the Auden tradition. Lewis, with his conscience being seared by various fires, was dealing more directly with his own psychology, hence Thomas's influence. He was also advised by Robert Graves – which may not have been such a good thing. Lewis's successful poems tend to be the longer, self-meditative yet sharply observant poems. His attempts at lyric and song-like forms, particularly some of the love lyrics, are less than convincing.

The beginning of the struggle in his poetic work may be shown by 'Prologue: the Grinder', the introductory poem to his first book *Raiders' Dawn*.

> I grind my words like knives on such events
> As I encounter in my peddling round.
> But the worn whetstone's whirling face prevents
> The perfect statement of the truths I found.

It was that worn whetstone he struggled to mend and finally he made it work less intermittently than when he began. All the elements of the struggle are in those lines; the gypsy-like romanticism of the wandering peddler, the second line's emphasis on personal experience and the last's reference to working away at clear statements of truths, a word the ironic modern tradition was chary of.

The issue is again put in the second verse of the uncollected poem 'On the Welsh Mountain':

> Deliberately to understate:
> To pare down to the quick
> Reality; to be
> In love articulate.

The poem indicates the whole struggle. The opening verse presents a turning away from Wales in nature to be more moved by the deprivation, debris and wreckage of Welsh life caused by industrialisation – but not in any external Audenesque way, though the odd Auden trick or two occur randomly in his work.

The third verse speaks of being forced to imagine something more romantic as its lines try to evoke mermaid and lover in the siren language that always could tempt him:

> Till my fingers
> Lambent in her maiden hair,
> Play simple strange
> Chromatic scales.

– He tended to shift into this rather poetic romantic phrasing when irreconcilable pressures pushed him into escape or shelve-it motion. The speaker finally turns away from 'a lost age'. Presumably this was the age of pre-industrial Wales.

The things that helped him to resolve his whetstone problem were three-fold. The developing skill of his own prose in the short stories and draft novels rubbed off on the poems, his army experience, and the previously mentioned influence of Edward Thomas, another poet of Anglo-Celtic origins, who died in war, and whose work gave support to Lewis's introspective yet also objective methods. Thomas also had that darker attraction for Lewis in sharing his own suicidal undercurrents. But Thomas also helped to enable him to bring the directness of his prose into the concerns dominating his verse and enabled him more fully to trust his own responses to experience; the army forced him inescapably into facing experience directly. Compared with Douglas, his poems reveal a wider sympathy for the common lot of people and soldiers, a result of his ameliorist propensities. Yet those sympathies received powerful shocks in the barracks where he encountered close-up the milieu of working-class language and behaviour. As he wrote in italic to close the introductory poem quoted first above:

> Keep grinding then although nothing's left to whet –
> Bad luck unless your sparks can warm the night.

Poems like 'After Dunkirk' reveal his growing doubts about the possibilities that ameliorist social approaches might be left with under the effects of war and the 'subterfuges of democracy'.

The phrase 'lost age' that closes 'On the Welsh Mountain' also concludes 'The Mountain over Aberdare' where the scarcely imagined girl of that first version becomes 'that white frock that floats down the dark alley ...'

In this version the romantic flight tendency towards the hills, the mermaid and the sea, Romantic diction and capitalization are firmly avoided. Later he could control this sort of diction better. He put it to powerful use in 'Goodbye' where ante- and penultimate verses in this diction, now with a degree of ironic emphasis on the personal pronouns, contrast with the-down-to-earth situation: the wish and the reality. Here are the last two verses:

> We made the universe to be our home,
> Our nostrils took the wind to be our breath,
> Our hearts are massive towers of delight,
> We stride across the seven seas of death.

> Yet when all's said and done you'll keep the emerald
> I placed upon your finger in the street;
> And I will keep the patches that you sewed
> On my old battledress tonight, my sweet.

(The 'seven seas' refer indirectly to embarkation.)

It is clear from 'The Mountain over Aberdare', and several other poems, that Lewis could not escape his Welshness, even if he had wanted to do so. Jeremy Hooker, in his *Selected Poems of Alun Lewis*, 1981, it seems to this reader, underplayed the Welsh aspects, or perhaps overplayed them, in suggesting that Lewis was trying to turn from the communal tradition of the arts and life of Wales to a more individualistic poetry like other modern poets. Yet Lewis's fellow-feelings for his Welsh soldiers in the rank and file made him hesitate to seek a commission. He eventually took officer-training and a commission against his better judgement, he thought. He was amazed his social abilities and conduct passed muster on the course among the other upper-class contenders while others were clearly turfed out for theirs. He still preferred to be with the Welsh rank and file with their songs and tales than among officers in their mess.

Just before his death, in 'Bequest', he is commending Gweno to the care of the Welsh in their communal culture.

> And these recur and I am glad
> That they have lived and died
> Within my blood and will live on
> Whatever may betide.

> I leave you in their company,
> The winter snow heaped on your door
> In the dark house in the mountains ...

About the same time, he also refused a staff position at base, when the regiment was to move into action, in order to be at the front with his men, despite his reluctance to kill a fellow-being. He also wanted to experience the heightened senses of the heat of battle.

India and the war brought to the forefront of his mind several inescapable pressures: the time was fast approaching to kill or be killed; ameliorist tendencies would not save the Indian peasant under the British domination that he was now committed to defend; his sense that strong personal love and commitment were vital was compromised by a love affair.

His work takes on a fascination with the Indian religions of fatalism and acceptance and an interest in ideas of the dark. The India experience develops what he observed in 'After Dunkirk':

> A growing self-detachment making man
> Less home-sick, fearful, proud,
> But less a man.
> Beneath all this
> The dark imagination that would pierce
> Infinite night and reach the waiting arms
> And soothe the guessed-at tears.

Such a conquest of self in India took on a more spiritual aspect for Lewis. He had no real belief in any conventional religion. His references to the darkness and night do not appear to approach something like the dark night of the soul. In discussing death with someone he was impressed not by any idea of an after-life of any sort but rather by the overwhelming thought of the peace that comes with the end of life's struggles. The one thing he does try to convince himself of is that what would be surviving is personal love in some nebulous platonic way. Some of his poems would like to 'prove', as Larkin put it, 'Our almost-instinct almost true:/ What will survive of us is love.'

But not always. In 'Water Music' he writes:

> Cold is the lake water
> And dark as history.
> Hurry not and fear not
> This oldest mystery.
>
> This strange voice singing,
> This slow deep drag of the lake,
> This yearning, yearning, this ending
> Of the heart and its ache.

In 'Burma Casualty' occurs a passage that brings to mind its similarity to the lines from 'After Dunkirk':

> The dark is a beautiful singing sexless angel
> Her hands so soft you scarcely feel her touch
> Gentle, eternally gentle, round your heart.
> She flatters and unsexes every man.

Though the poem is more or less a dramatic monologue, it is doing Lewis's usual thing of thinking through personal problems and experience by observing them in others. The last line above suggests that he is not convinced by the flattery of the dark angel.

Yet the idea of turning away from the world does not leave him:

> And when my sweetheart calls me shall I tell her
> That I am seeking less and less of world
> And will she understand?

he asks in 'Karanje Village'. He suggests in 'Shadows':

> He chooses best who does not choose
> Time and all its lies;
> Who makes the end and the beginning One
> Within himself, grows wise.

In his last poem, 'The Jungle'. he concludes:

> Or does the will's long struggle end
> With the last kindness of a foe or friend?

His work leaves these and many questions open. Jeremy Hooker suggested that the 'darkness' in his poems relates to Lewis's capitalized 'that which IS', of 'To Rilke' and calls it the ground of being. But the capitalization also occurs in the much earlier 'Westminster Abbey', written before arrival in India.

> And no one stays within that holy shell
> To know if that which IS be good or ill.

Nor does he seem to be referring to darkness as the mystery that all real poets know: the mysterious place in the psyche where poems develop.

The attempt at acceptance in these poems may have been influenced by the Indian religious tradition; but the darkness may often come close to the darkness that Edward Thomas courted. We cannot know. Nor did Lewis, I suspect, who struggled with such issues in his work. The fact is he wrote to Gweno while in India, saying: 'I find myself quite unable to express at once the passion of Love, the coldness of Death … and the fire that beats against resignation, acceptance. Acceptance seems so spiritless, protest so vain. In between the two I live.'

He was not given time to answer such questions and we should not attempt to be certain about them when Lewis, like Keats, lived in the poet's uncertainty. As the military inquiry recorded, he died before he saw action by an accident with his side-arm.

William Virgil Davis

The Poet-Priest

for R. S. Thomas (in memory)

He strove to make the meaning
mean, to show, and let it seem
to be by being.

Along the rain-draped hills
he strode to search and find
what needed finding.

He saw himself as first
example, cursed and cured,
crying out a silent shout,

standing in a road alone.
And when, the long way
walked, he turned his final

turn, a small bird stirred
ahead of him
and seemed to say

in notes almost no one
could hear: *here now*
begin again.

Stephen Devereux

The Contradictory Mr. Thomas

Read almost anything about R. S. Thomas and you are sure to come, very soon, upon the word 'contradictions.' Byron Rogers begins his *Guardian* obituary with 'He was the strangest bundle of contradictions.'[1] This bundle, we learn, includes his often contemptuous attitude towards his parishioners contradicting his Christian faith; said contempt negating his Welsh nationalism; his nationalism incompatible with his *English* wife and his *English* accent and his *English*-boarding-school-educated son and his *English* poetry and his pacifism undermined by his support for the fire-bombing of *English*-owned cottages in Wales. Yet, while Rogers explores these 'contradictions' with quotations from the poems as opposed to anecdotes from the life, to *read* Thomas's poetry without knowledge of the man (as I did the first time) is to experience almost a singularity of vision, language and intent that comes from the reading of very few other post-Victorian poets. Almost – because that unity of vision is, arguably, the most contradictory aspect of Thomas's work.

Thomas is also a mirror in which the gazer sees their own preoccupations. Religious readers interpret his work in terms of a consistent programme and compare him with Herbert and Vaughan; Welsh nationalists identify his voice closely with their voice and readers of nature poetry see him as part of that well established line from Wordsworth, through Hardy and Hughes to Heaney and MacCaig. That Thomas could be seen as a representative figure of so many kinds of poetry is yet another contradiction to add to the tally, and one that has generated numerous attempts to find appropriate definitions for his work and for his contribution to British verse.

Michael Schmidt[2] considers the sobriquet 'Christian realist' but soon rejects it for the narrower 'poet-clergyman,' particularly as a means of exploring the earlier poems. This definition is one Thomas shares with George Crabbe and there are a surprising number of comparisons between them: both poets 'inherited' their forms and took them for granted; both wrote about the lives of their grim parishioners in equally grim terms; both used the role of the priest as a device to describe the lives of their subjects; both generate a particular, unlovely landscape in which to place the people and incidents they describe. Compare Thomas's Iago Prytherch with Crabbe's Peter Grimes:

> So are his days spent, his spittled mirth
> Rarer than the sun that cracks the cheeks
> Of the gaunt sky perhaps once a week.
> And then at night see him fixed in his chair
> Motionless, except when he leans to gob in the fire.
> 'A Peasant', 1955

Thus by himself compell'd to live each day,
To wait for certain hours the tide's delay;
At the same time the same dull views to see,
The bounding marsh-bank and the blighted tree.

The Parish Register, 1807

In both poems the lone individuals are presented as if watched closely by an unseen observer, emphasising their separateness. Each is part of a morose harmony between individual and landscape, unwished for and evident only to the observer. Neither Crabbe nor Thomas recognises their own humanity in these isolated figures. This is very unlike the Romantics' striving for an active and positive connection between figure, landscape and observer and from Vaughan's mystic, emblematic use of the lone figure in a landscape, such as in 'Regeneration.'

Grimes is heading for damnation, of course, and the phantasms will rise out of the river from which he cannot escape to damn him; whereas Prytherch must trudge on across his dull, wet hillside, judged only by his creator. And here, perhaps, is the source of a significant contradiction in Thomas's project: Crabbe relies on the Enlightenment filtered through Christian morality to give closure to the lives of his rustics (his strongest condemnation is of the vicar who leaves a pauper unblessed in his grave): Thomas must push his taciturn hill farmers towards a *political* resolution rather than to salvation or purgatory. In 'Invasion on the Farm' Prytherch must be given his 'own' voice, rather than being the poem's dumb subject. The outsider is no longer the invisible watcher but the (presumably English) intruder. Prytherch's language, his slow thoughts, his 'crude fingers' establish a physical connection between the figure and his landscape as a contrast to the fleeting visitor who leaves the gate open to let in the 'cold winds of the world.' The relationship between the 'peasant' and his country/landscape is a fixed one, but is vulnerable to the greater force of the ungrounded race of invaders. In order to make this contrast a political statement, Thomas must have Prytherch articulate his mute connection with the essence of his country: 'the old farm/Warm as a sack about me' and this capacity to voice his symbolic purpose weakens our sense of his identity.

Time and again, the superbly realised representation of the Welsh landscape and its expression through the lives of its inhabitants, is vulnerable and inactive in the face of erosion and colonisation. Such a depiction does not lend itself easily to politicisation. To give a voice to what is unvoiced through a less artificial device, Thomas elsewhere resorts to myth and history. In 'Taliesin 1952,' Wales's most ancient poet is given a powerful voice that subsumes those of the country's political and spiritual heroes. He has been Merlin, Glyn Dwr, Goronwy and in the present will 'Show you a new world, risen,/Stubborn with beauty, out of the heart's need.' This stubborn beauty, present throughout history, arises out of necessity, out of the people's need for it, like the sleeping dragon, the mythological avenger who will sweep all contamination, all foreign elements from the sacred soil. The effect is of a stupendous rhetorical climax rather than Prytherch's muted pleas to be left undisturbed behind his closed gate. But who is the intended audience for this sublime polemic? Should we read it as a warning to the English/urban/tourist/cottage-buying outsider? As a prophetic poem it is decidedly anaemic when compared with Gray's Bard, who calls not only upon the poetic and political heroes of Wales, but also on the Old Testament prophets, to put a curse upon the English monarchy. He 'repairs the golden flood' (of poetry and nationhood) by his sacrifice: 'headlong from the mountain's height/Deep in the roaring tide he plunged to endless night.' And for Gray, two hundred years before Thomas, this was merely an exercise, an attempt to create the perfect Pindaric ode, rather than a statement of a deeply held political belief. Perhaps Taliesin's ambiguity stems from the impossibility, in the twentieth century, of making statements of vengeful nationalism – at least in reference to those long yoked words England and Wales. Or should we see the audience for the poem as, rather, an interior one, a call not so much to the peasantry, but to the custodians of Welsh culture to initiate a new golden age? If so, then the poem makes its plea more by the example of its own language, by its conjuring up of a stubborn beauty, by the rhythms of the names it recites, than by creating a stirring call to arms or suggesting *how* such a resurgence might come about.

In 'A Welshman to Any Tourist' the voices of the bard and the peasant are replaced by a kind of collective Welsh voice, one that is almost apologetic for the lack of (apparently) overtly appealing attractions in the Welsh landscape. The poem concludes with the idea that King Arthur and his knights 'are the bright ore/That seams our history,/But shame has kept them late in bed.' The dragon/avenging giant sleeps because his people are not worthy of him – they must become worthy before he will awake. And here lies another inconsistency – Taliesin was being called upon to awaken the Welsh from their slumber: Arthur sleeps because his people are not ready for him. Should this sleeping Arthur be the ultimate attraction for 'any tourist'? As a symbol of nationhood to both the English and the Welsh this *could* suggest that the poem is actually an attempt at conciliation. Or is the tone more ironic, suggesting that what is ultimately of value in Wales (its 'ore') is its latent nationhood, a force that will drive the invaders out whilst becoming irresistible to tourists?

It is when Thomas eschews the overtly political that any contradictions in tone and message fade. In another poem about a sleeping giant, 'The Survivor,' the clergyman-poet stance facilitates writing of tremendous power, vitality and certainty. Its opening: 'Yesterday I found one left' is colloquial and like an entry in a journal or notebook. We anticipate the elegiac, a tribute to the last representative of the nation's lost values. Instead we a given an incisive portrait of a dying bully. He is no longer capable of 'mischief' only because he is too old. His weakness has leant him 'a brief/Time for repenting' that would have been denied him had he died with his boots on. And what he must repent is his 'theft/Of health and comeliness from her/Who lay caught in his strong arms.' A brutal sexuality is suggested, not only by these lines but by the association of man with animal through the 'beasts' who 'moan and stir.' A gross, inverted nativity scene is evoked. The survivor is 'The land's thug,' a 'bundle of fat and bone.' The land is feminised, 'Lovely as the eye could wish/in its green clothes', but is 'beaten black/ And blue by the deeds of dour men'. In the imperatives of the final stanza, it is the priest in Thomas who orders 'Wake him up. It is too late/Now for the blood's foolish dreaming.' He 'must chew now/The cud of prayer and be taught how/ From hard hearts huge tears are wrung.' The animal imagery is sustained and it is now the voice of the chapel rather than the church that curses the old man for his bestial excesses. No Christian consolation through repentance is suggested, merely the punishment of contemplating his life, made possible by the stay of execution given him by a 'strange grace.' And yet this survivor rises through the language of the poem like a standing stone, a more primitive and fecund version of Prytherch (Prick/Earth). His power is increased rather than diminished by the priest's disapproval. Before he was brought low, he took his power from his nation's myths, from the 'blood's foolish dreaming.' The bathos/pathos of his last days that the poet-clergyman leaves us with, is overshadowed by the force of his brutal figure.

'Reservoirs' is another poem that takes its power from a sense of revulsion, but succeeds in being overtly political without apparent contradiction. Once again, Thomas beguiles us with a colloquial, confessional opening 'There are places in Wales I don't go.' The second line develops simultaneously both the literal and metaphorical meanings of 'reservoirs' with the assertion that they are the 'subconscious/Of a people'. Then, in a typical Thomas shift, he moves back to the literal with '[they are] troubled far down/With gravestones, chapels, villages even.' Just as a people's conscience is troubled by its failure to stop whole communities being destroyed to make way for reservoirs that will supply English cities with water, so the Welsh psyche is troubled by its disrupted history and by the indignity of the conquered. Through the intense association of ideas that is the hallmark of Thomas's best writing, the conceit of the depths of the water representing the hidden aspects of the mind is extended into the comparison of the water's surface with a face. For a neo-romantic poet, this would inevitably lead to a consolatory personification, but Thomas breaks away to a sudden interjection: 'The serenity of their [reservoirs] expression/Revolts me.' The 'expression' on the face of the waters is hypocritical, it denies the graves that lie in its depths, it is a 'pose for strangers.' The weight of the line then moves us effortlessly towards the question of representation. The reflective surface of the reservoir has 'a watercolour's appeal/ To the mass, instead of the poem's/Harsher conditions.' The poem/poet must penetrate the illusion, resist the temptation of popular culture, remain the isolated visionary. As if still looking at a painting the view shifts to the surrounding hills. These too are desecrated by the 'scum/Of the forests.' In language that evokes the violence of conquest, the farms also have faces, faces that have been 'smashed,' bringing together in this image the desecrations that took place in the past with the current devastation by the water companies of Liverpool and Manchester. As happens sometimes in Thomas's verse, the power of this image is weakened by the redundant comparison of the stones of the farms spreading down the hillside with tears. Perhaps he couldn't quite trust his readers to add that detail in their imaginations.

In the second stanza, the 'I' of the poem is now *in* the scene, 'walk[ing] the shore/For an hour' (but hadn't he told us at the beginning that he doesn't go to such places?). The battle/invasion imagery continues with the 'English/ Scavenging among the remains/Of our culture.' The poem ends by accusing the Welsh ('we') of complicity in the pillaging- 'elbowing our language/Into the grave that we have dug for it.' We discover that the 'graves' hidden at the bottom of the reservoirs and in the 'subconscious/Of a people' are actually the guilty secrets of self-immolation.

'Reservoirs' achieves what none of the other political poems quite achieve. There is a remarkably tight cohesion of image, metaphor and argument into a recursive poem that, at the final moment, turns the revulsion expressed throughout the poem away from the aggression of the invaders and against the people who, not only fail to resist, but hide their failure in the depths – of their subconscious, of their history and of their landscape. But that brilliant cohesion presents us with another contradiction: Thomas's poems create an aesthetic of defeat, of misery, of ravaged landscapes that is more memorable than the people and the country that are the poems' subjects, whereas Crabbe pities, moralises, excuses, condemns and is, primarily interested in the humanity of his subjects. They serve no purpose for him beyond the lessons they provide. There is nothing beautiful about his drunken youth who must marry his pregnant girlfriend and live out a life of predictable brutality, poverty and hardship. He is typical, rather than representative; his connection with his landscape is economic rather than symbolic. The closely observed situation is what the reader remembers. Thomas gives us pictures – sometimes still lives, sometimes movies.

While it would be unjust to accuse Thomas of not caring for the subjects of his poems, *as humans,* their humanity is not what generates his best poetry. In 'The Face' the figure in the landscape is reduced both by his literal distance up the hillside from the observer and through his recreation in the observer's imagination 'When I close my eyes, I can see it,/The bare hill with the man ploughing'. The figure is immediately objectified and the opening 'When' almost suggests that it is only through the imagination that this figure can be fully realised. The second stanza reaffirms the ploughman's status as symbol or myth 'He is never absent, but like a slave/Answers to the mind's bidding'. His eyes are the colour of rain and 'He is like bark/Weathering on the tree of his kind.' The title becomes ironic, since we are never given *his* face - only the face of the landscape, of which he has become an expression. The poem ends with a picture, a framed one that will be hung on the 'walls/Of the mind's gallery'. The poem is as much about Thomas' poetry as it is about the lone ploughman (who, if he ever existed, probably longed for a council house full of the modcons Thomas despised and a job indoors). The poem describes the process by which an external image is removed from its context, given an enormous (and always available) symbolic weight and kept, like a trophy in the mind's memory bank. There is no desire to return to the actual figure at the end of the poem, but to the framed, unchanging image. Wordsworth was equally interested in the 'mind's eye,' but there is always an urge, as in 'Tintern Abbey' to return, to check that the image matches the memory, to compare the memory of the same scene on different occasions. Thomas, having created his masterpiece, is content to hang it inside his skull.

Ultimately, though, Thomas's contradictions arise out of the size of his canvas. He is not a Crabbe, writing detailed narratives about the lives of the rural poor. Nor is he a Wordsworth, processing the landscape and its inhabitants through his 'egotistical sublime.' He is most certainly not a Protestant mystic transforming his figures and landscapes into an all-encompassing language of prophecy, nor a nature poet, content to zoom in on the minutiae of life. He tries, magnificently, to create a language out of the mythical and the real, out of a nation's suffering and its glories, out of polemics and unforgettable images. The contradictions come with the territory, are an essential part of that language.

[1] *The Guardian,* 27.09.2000
[2] Michael Schmidt, *An Introduction to Fifty Modern British Poets,* Pan, 1979, p.261

W S Milne

Omnium Gatherum of Welsh Books

Tony Curtis, *After the First Death: an Anthology of Wales and War in the Twentieth Century,* Seren Books, £9.99 paperback

Tony Curtis, *Wales at War: Critical Essays on Literature and Art*, Seren Books, £14.99

Gwyneth Lewis, *Chaotic Angels: Poems in English*, Bloodaxe Books, £9.95 paperback

Glyn Hughes, *Two Marriages*, Shoestring Press, £7.00 paperback

Glyn Hughes, *Dancing Out Of The Dark Side*, Shoestring Press, £8.95 paperback

Glenys Jones, *In the beginning was the song*, Matador, £6.99 paperback

Ian Davidson, *As if only*, Shearsman Books, £7.99 paperback

Zoë Skoulding, *Remains of a Future City*, Seren Books, £7.99 paperback

Paul Henry, *Ingrid's Husband*, Seren Books, £7.99 paperback

Sheenagh Pugh, *Long-Haul Travellers*, Seren Books, £7.99 paperback

Peter Riley, *The Llŷn Writings*, Shearsman Books £8.99 paperback

Peter Riley, *The Day's Final Balance: Uncollected Writings 1965-2006*, Shearsman Books, £9.99

Steve Griffith, *Landing*, Rack Press, £4 paperback

Byron Beynon, *Cuffs*, Rack Press, £4 paperback

Patrick McGuinness, *19ᵗʰ Century Blues,* Smith/Doorstop Books, £3

John Powell Ward, *Variations On Four Places*, Rack Press, £5 paperback

Ruth Bidgood, *Time Being*, Seren Books, £7.99 paperback

Deryn Rees-Jones, *Falls & Finds*, Shoestring Press, £5 paperback

Samantha Wynne-Rhydderch, *Not In These Shoes,* Picador Poetry, £8.99 paperback

Peter Finch, *The Welsh Poems*, Shearsman Books, £9.95 paperback

Meirion Jordan, *Moonrise,* Seren Books, £7.99

Andrew McNeillie, *Slower*, Carcanet, £9.95 paperback

A linguistic point to begin with. None of these books or pamphlets is written in the Welsh language but they are all, nevertheless, determinedly Welsh in spirit. The position of the Welsh poet writing in English today (or indeed of any Celt, be they Scottish, Irish, Manx, Welsh, Cornish or Breton – what Hugh MacDiarmid called 'the Celtic crescent') is similar to those authors composing a rich literature in Irish through the fifteenth to the seventeenth centuries in the Highlands and Islands of Scotland. Although they were writing what seemed like a foreign language to some, Irish did not prevent these Scotsmen and Scotswomen from praising their own geographical and political homeland. And so it is here. It is perfectly possible to sing of Wales in the tongue of the coloniser.

Tony Curtis's two books are companion volumes, composed almost like a diptych. They bring together the best of poetry and prose written in English by Welsh authors, or by authors associated with Wales in some way, and critical essays on some of those writers. The title of the first book of course comes from Dylan Thomas's great elegy on the London Blitz (he in fact wrote six poems in total on this theme, all published in his 1946 volume, *Deaths and Entrances*), 'A Refusal to Mourn, the Death by Fire, of a Child in London', and there is a fine essay in the accompanying volume by James A. Davie arguing that the theme of conflict is prevalent throughout Thomas's work, 'for Thomas never escaped an obsession with war and the violence of wars. It is at the heart of his literary achievement' (a theme partially picked up on in John Maybury's 2008 film on the poet, *The Edge of Love*). It is extremely interesting to note just how many Welsh writers have chosen warfare as their theme. The anthology contains some of the best known names, such as David Jones, Vernon Watkins, Alun Lewis, Robert Graves (he was commissioned in a Welsh regiment), Wilfred Owen (he had Welsh ancestors), Edward Thomas, and R S Thomas, but also a considerable number of fine, lesser known authors, all writers of conscience, disdainful of jingoism and ready to oppose false notions of war. The inclusion of Ivor Gurney seems rather tenuous, however, great poet though he is (he makes mention of 'a Welsh colony' in his poem 'First Time In'). I suppose such eclecticism is no wider of the mark than the strategies adopted by the managers of national football teams! I was also surprised by Curtis's opening remark that 'Owen was...perhaps the greatest poet of any war'. It is probably true to say that Owen is the most articulate of the First World War poets (although both Rosenberg and Gurney run him close seconds) but surely Keith Douglas is at least his equal in the Second? And, if you take the long view, surely Homer must be given the accolade overall. There is a fine selection of poems by Alun Lewis, indubitably one of the very finest of the Second World War poets, and in the second book there are fine essays on Alun Lewis himself, David Jones, and R S Thomas by Duncan Campbell, Cary Archard (who edited Alun Lewis's *Collected Poems* for Seren in 2007: see Peter Dale's review of that book in this issue) and M. Wynn Thomas respectively. There is a very detailed essay on war in the writings of Llewelyn Wyn Griffith, Robert Graves (mainly on *Goodbye to All That*), Wilfred Owen (and his early interest in Welsh history in a poem such as 'Uriconium: An Ode') and Edward Thomas (and his deep reading of the Welsh epic, *The Mabinogion*, and its effect upon his work) by Jeremy Hooker. The book is worth buying for this essay alone. Hooker is particularly illuminating on Griffith's *Up to Mametz*, a book that matches the spirit of David Jones's much better known *In Parenthesis*. The scale of the psychological diremption caused by the First World War can be witnessed in Griffith's telling phrase that that war 'threw a doubt upon all meaning in words.' Both books encapsulate that terror of war which Edward Thomas describes memorably, and drawing, as Tony Curtis expresses it, 'from the depths of European mythology', particularly from Dante's Hell, 'The unfathomable deep / Forest, where all must lose / their way.' It is strange, however, I feel, that there is no mention made of the effect on the Welsh language itself of the two world wars. Tony Conran, for example, in his Introduction to *The Penguin Book of Welsh Verse*, blames these catastrophes, together with the Great Depression, for reducing the number of Welsh speakers in the land, the rot having set in, he believes, in even earlier, Elizabethan times. Notwithstanding this, Tony Curtis's books on warfare and Wales in the twentieth century carry great conviction from a poet who is himself included in the anthology. One of the riches here is the inclusion of prose works. It is one of the unchallenged assumptions of literature that the Welsh are poets only. The Celts, as Kenneth Hurlstone Jackson pointed out some years ago, are also great masters of imaginative prose composition and narrative, and the selections here gathered sensitively and emphatically reinforce that fact. These volumes are timely, given the number of wars being fought on different fronts across the world today.

Gwyneth Lewis was the first writer to be made the official National Poet of Wales, in 2005, in much the same manner as Edwin Morgan was confirmed Scotland's first national poet, The Scots Makar, in 2004, both positions rivalling that of The Poet Laureate in England, and clearly symbolising the political struggle for self-autonomy in both countries, partly achieved through the establishing of The Welsh Assembly and The Scottish Parliament. Lewis's fluency in Welsh and English represents that condition of 'antisyzygy', or combination of opposites, G. Gregory Smith observed in the Caledonian character in his 1919 book on Scottish Literature (and further extended by Hugh MacDiarmid in his critiques of James Hogg and R. L. Stevenson), the oxymoronic task of straddling two horses at the same time, of mastering two languages imaginatively (Edwin Muir famously thought the task impossible). I am not qualified enough to comment on Lewis's Welsh poems, but the English poems brought together here by the joint efforts of Bloodaxe Books and the Welsh Books Council are certainly of a high calibre. The effect of her poems is to remind me of Seamus Heaney's earlier poetic excavations into the Celtic past, and how that tradition still flourishes simultaneously in the Mother Tongue of the Celt and in the foreign *koinē* (one could hardly call it a dialect) of English. This bi-lingual mix (sometimes conscious, sometimes not) lies at the heart, I am certain, of much Celtic literature, as in the work of Yeats, Joyce, MacDiarmid, David Jones, Sorley MacLean, George Campbell Hay, and Seamus Heaney himself. The confluence of two literary cultures creates spiritual and intellectual upheavals which, in turn, forge new artistic directions. The work of Gwyneth Lewis belongs I feel to that innovative tradition.

Glyn Hughes is an exiled Welshman living in the Pennines. His two books of verse demonstrate a deep understanding of the Celtic legacy of nature writing. The observational detail is very precise and pointed in his work:

> Now a numinous image flakes
> from a broken wall
> where the peasant and his mule
> plough with crooked sticks
> around forgotten runics
> with a soft football.

He also shares with Gwyneth Lewis a stance of gentle Christian humanism, of learning's 'torch of flame' (see Lewis's lines, 'Christ brings cool docks of mercy', 'Novalis knew / that all illness requires a musical cure') beyond R. S. Thomas's severe Kierkegaardianism (what Geoffrey Hill calls his 'sacramental nihilism', and

Rowan Williams his 'uneasy faith', his 'experience of living over dark fathoms'). Hughes's humour, however, seems more profound than hers, deeper in its application, and grounded in the genius of locality:

I feel like warm moist sleepy earth,
the soil of Edens longed and lusted for:
religion's memories; explorers' desires.

His pastoralism is rooted in an appreciation of the long western tradition, beginning with Greece (in 'House'), though, again, like Gwyneth Lewis, he does dwell briefly at one point on pre-history, in 'Petralona Man', through Middle English Literature to John Taverner, Milton, Charlotte Brontë, Donizetti, Chekhov, Van Gogh, L. S. Lowry and Ted Hughes. There is a mystical element present in these poems which has affinities with the poetry of John Burnside. *Two Marriages* is an autobiographical poem, a very difficult form, probably best practised in modern times by Basil Bunting in *Briggflatts* and by Geoffrey Hill in *Mercian Hymns*. At times I felt that the poetry was too close to prose, but the structure of the narrative, nevertheless, is successful and tight, reminding me of Whitley Stokes's categorisation of Celtic literature as being strongly defined, realistic and logical in design. The reason for this is best articulated by the poet himself who argues in a preface that 'Naturalism is a shallow creed, yet through a careful desire for subjective truth, art's deeper concerns –the archetypes, and the mysteries, art as a window on another world—may take care of themselves, if one has anything to express about them.' *Dancing Out of the Dark Side*, nevertheless, is the more successful of the two books. I particularly enjoyed reading 'Foxes', 'Stones', 'Bride Stones', 'Listening to Larks', and 'The Centipede'. They have something of the fresh concision of the *englynion* where intelligence and feeling meet like sparks. The poet also illustrates his own books, as David Jones did, and the quality of the artwork matches that of the verse, with the book-covers being particularly fine.

Glenys Jones heads up her book with a fine quotation from Kingsley Amis: 'whatever a poem may be, it is not just a text on a page but also a part of somebody's life.' This observation certainly applies to her own work where the traditional motif of *hiraeth* (usually translated weakly into English as 'homesickness', but more clearly defined by Val Bethell as 'the link with the long-forgotten past, the language of the soul, the call from the inner self', *BBC Wales*, March 2003) is particularly well worked out in the poem of that title, and in 'Love Deferred', 'Camelot' and 'And Are There Paintings Still For Tea?' These are courageous achievements for a poet who suffers from chronic fatigue syndrome, whose 'energy resources', as she terms them, are often circumscribed. The sense of *hiraeth*, then, of spiritual longing, makes of Jones's poetry a contemplative and expressive exercise in the arena of language and belonging. Amis's words are pertinent in this context, and reminded me of Rush Rhees's estimation of Wittgenstein's philosophy: 'Language goes with a way of living', 'Wittgenstein used to say that to imagine a language is to imagine a form of life' (in *Discussions of Wittgenstein*, 1970), the way of living here, of course, being Welsh.

Hiraeth is also very strong in Ian Davidson's work. Although he may be writing in Barcelona, in London, or on the Baltic coast, in Fez, or in Marrakech, Wales is never very far away from Ian Davidson's heart. In his Introduction to the book he phrases this fierce attraction to home as 'How the traces of a life had marked the skin.' Of the poems I liked 'moon and mist matters' and 'Seas of flags' for their close imagism and feeling, though I was puzzled as to why so many titles were unnecessarily (as it seems to me) in lower case letters. We must thank the Welsh Academy and Arts Council England for finding the money to help Shearsman Books bring out this, Davidson's fourth collection of verse.

Zoë Skoulding has collaborated with Ian Davidson in the past, on a poetry collection, and their work is in many ways not dissimilar, sharing an interest in Christian humanist mysticism, especially the work of Marsilio Ficino and Tommaso Campanella. Her poetry looks out from North Wales onto the languages of Europe –those of Denmark, the Low Countries, Germany, the Balkans— with an understanding of diverse cultures made tangible in experimental typographical forms. 'The lines of the language' she says, 'run through to me to somewhere else', making of her work an internationalist poetics.

Paul Henry is from Aberystwyth and came to poetry through song-writing, a long-established Celtic tradition. There is an authentic sense of abstract thought and solid realism finely balanced in his poetry which reminded me at times of the best of W. S. Graham, finding epiphanies in a Welsh setting as Graham often did in Cornwall and Greenock, and a feeling of exile from something that once nourished the roots of language itself:

> Shall we stay then, love?
> It's only the years moving inside us
> and everything hurts in autumn.
> Where shall we put them,
> the years, in our new house?
> the years we are moving out of?

His poems possess the unpretentious clarity and directness Kenneth Allott found in the 1930s' English poet Bernard Spencer (the epigraph to Henry's book is from Spencer's poem, 'On The Road'), intelligently reflecting on his perceptions and apprehensions. Henry is a very fine poet.

Like Skoulding and Henry, Sheenagh Pugh's concerns are global, whether lauding Antony Gormley's sculptural work in the North West of England, the thirteenth century Icelandic *Poetic Edda*, the Roman fort at South Shields, the Dutch privateer Murat Reis, Paul Hunter at the Welsh Open golf championship in 1996, or invocations of Leningrad and Trondheim. My favourite poems were 'The Unconversations', praising a married couple's silent communion, and her elegy to the Orkney poet, George Mackay Brown. Like him she carves her words to last without sacrificing the fluency of life behind them. Skoulding, Henry and

Pugh's poetry evinces that fine quality of light which makes you feel while it lasts a special sense of freedom the Highlands novelist Neil Gunn writes of in his work. The Welsh Books Council and Seren Press must be praised for the high quality of book design and production evident in all three volumes.

Like Ian Davidson, Peter Riley's books are published by Shearsman Books of Exeter. Both *The Llŷn Writings* and *The Day's Final Balance* collate poetry and prose pieces, the first concentrating on texts composed on annual visits to the Llŷn Peninsula in North Wales between 1977 and 1998 (not simply 'holiday' poems though, but poems of place 'where topography and meditation meet' as the information on the back of the book puts it), the second containing a new extension to his long poem, *Alstonefield,* and a collection of one-hundred-and-eighteen short, epigrammatic poems. The epigraph to *The Day's Final Balance* is from Francis Ponge, and the Frenchman's influence is detectable at times in the volume, in the focus on quotidian matter for example:

> The snow-melt late this year. High up, big patches of snow still
> Remaining, perilous uncertainties across the paths, upper surfaces
> Crusted and pitted, sometimes concealing quite big streams,
> Which you can hear passing under the snow.

He is writing here of the Alps, though it could equally well be of Snowdonia. I especially enjoyed 'From Poems to Pictures by Jack B. Yeats', the Celtic influence again shining through, and his 'derivations' (his own term for translations) from Mandelstam, Bobrowski, Montale, Machado and from Ponge himself (a version of 'Sombre période', in *Liasse*), the latter stressing the 'constancy and liberty' which 'guide our steps.' It was comforting to see an elegy for the unjustly neglected North Eastern English poet, Barry MacSweeney, and one for Ivor Gurney, a poet already noted above. The most significant section, or division, of *The Llŷn Writings* is the sequence entitled 'Sea Watches' (first published by Carcanet in *Passing Measures,* 2000) which looks back to the ancient Welsh tradition of employing complex rhyme schemes. In an afterword the author informs us that the end-rhymes 'are twelve lines apart and cannot without difficulty be held in the reader's memory. Their function is thus structural rather than melodic.' Here we have the classic Welsh craftsman at work in his poetry, defining his aesthetic within the context of a clear architectonic structure. Such dedication reminds one of the fourteen year apprenticeships served once by bards in the old Celtic schools. If only there were more such skilled craftsmen at work with words in this dystopian age! Linked to 'Sea Watches' are the sections 'Sea Watch Overstock' and 'The Translations of St. Columba's Sea-Watch' (which has also been translated by Kenneth Hurlstone Jackson and Edwin Morgan), the last again indicating the close cohesion of Celtic culture, be it Brythonic, or Irish, or Scottish Gaelic. Here is a book then which praises the sea's 'continual singing', 'the local waves beating on the rocks', and 'the sea's entire calm', whilst recognising Iona's affiliation with Wales:

We are established at the outer edge
Cloaked in brightness

This Celtic sensitivity to natural phenomena is also evident in Steve Griffiths's pamphlet, *Landing*, most especially in the poem 'Spring', and in Byron Beynon's *Cuffs* (another fine Rack Press pamphlet), particularly in the title poem and in 'Thrift', 'Rhossili Down' and in 'The Sound Return':

The tide has turned its face
from the shore, once more
the herring-gulls feed and quarrel
on the luminous mud
where lonely boats, abandoned and still,
wait, listening for the sound
return of the sea that will come
like the end of a journey.

We can hear St. Columba's voice yet in such a meditation, where prayer and its rhythmical pointing are both made equally clear.

As with Peter Riley, the French influence is strong in Patrick McGuinness's work (he is an established translator of Mallarmé). Such diverse figures as Monet, Flaubert, Baudelaire, Rimbaud and Rilke (in his French phase) and Christian Dotremont feature in his new pamphlet, and although I agree with Justin Quinn to a certain extent that McGuinness's translations from the French account for what he calls 'the different acoustics of his poetry', I feel also at the same time that his Welsh inheritance must not be underestimated. In his hands, for example, Baudelaire's 'Spleen' becomes the very contemporary 'Cardiff Matchday Blues', the French poet's Parisian correspondences metamorphosed into 'steel glades / whose girdered glass matches the angle of the rain.' Likewise, Rimbaud's 'Voyelles' is transmogrified into a northern chapel setting where 'the last Trumpet's strange and strident call' is heard, reminding one perhaps a little of John Martin's Victorian Apocalyptic paintings. The landscapes pictured here are of transient places such as airports, hotels, bars, stadia, holiday beaches where marriages are splitting up and where alcoholics have their third drink of the morning. They are such places that have exploded 'all our privacies', demonstrating a 'pell-mell' age with no spiritual or cultural 'ballast'. McGuinness shows that this shakiness has its foundations in the nineteenth century's 'discovery' of relativism (although not mentioned by him, one bears in mind Walter Pater's words of 1866, that 'to the modern spirit nothing is, or can be rightly known except relatively'). For example, in his poem 'The Shape Of Nothing Happening' (a very Beckettian title), McGuinness represents this feeling in the very bald assertion that 'there are no absolutes, that all is graded on the scale, / that all is incremental, deciduous, and undecided.' It is at this point that the seemingly awkward and arbitrary title of his pamphlet, *19th Century Blues*, begins to make sense. The artists listed above all in their own ways prefigured this epoch of disorientation and fragmentariness – what Dotremont described as 'Dépoésie' and McGuinness translates as 'Dispoetry.' McGuinness is hopeful, however, that art can survive all these upheavals, finding in words 'alchemy's / Stamp of peace on wrinkled studious brows.' His own artistic strategies bear out his optimism, based as they are on an alert awareness of the two-edged nature of reality, of 'Two tenses grappling with one instant, one perception' as he phrases it, and his acute eye discerning the Heraclitean evanescence of things, their clamour, 'the way / a shell holds / a recording of the waves even as the waves turn around it', 'the grainy, detailed hours have reached their zenith, / now they fall away', 'so your gentle hands / knew in advance / they were scales that weighed / the fullest of our hours', humankind viewed as

> Minnows caught in the slipstreams of their own stories,
> they tremble for a moment upcurrent, they are gone
> into the next instalment, the next word.

It is this very fluidity the artist tries to capture in his work, though 'Somewhere the Angel of Oblivion, radiant, leans his face into the wind / that turns our pages.' Patrick McGuinness is a very fine poet whose work demonstrates Pater's dictum that 'A faculty for truth is a power of distinguishing and fixing delicate and fugitive details.' My only surprise was that amongst McGuinness's list of nineteenth century French heroes he did not include Balzac whose *La Comédie humaine* surely presents us with the greatest nineteenth century example of the inexhaustible flow and brokenness of human life – a great work of art that prefigures all later developments.

John Powell Ward has written critical studies of R. S. Thomas and Wordsworth, and their influence is noticeable to a certain extent in his pamphlet, *Variations On Four Places*, but only again in the 'centrifugal' (the word is his own) sense of exile from a cherished place, be it Gower, Radnor, Somerset or Gloucester, 'the dream's resting-place', 'the single light' of belonging. For him, the feeling of *hiraeth* is particularly strong, stating 'Where to live' is 'the hardest / Decision there is' – the difficulty, as he sees it, of finding a locus to 'put down / New taproot without unclogging the old.' The sense of moving away from one's roots is anchored technically however in a sequence which is closely organised (each of the four parts of the poem, for example, is further sub-divided into eight sections) so that the poet can manage what might otherwise be his amorphous materials. This skilful restraint enables him to avoid any possible nostalgia or sentimentality which the poem might otherwise generate. The aim of the poet, he says, is to pull 'the clay from the ditch.' Although he makes large claims for poetry ('A spacious arch where certainties could free / The huge love essenced') he also sensibly guesses at its limitations, writing, rather like the American poet Marianne Moore, that 'there is more even than this, and so much more' – 'silence purer than water', 'the ancient purples and browns of autumn', the freedom of 'the wild ponies…Still not broken in…unnamed.'

Ruth Bidgood also writes of place, mid-Wales in particular. Perception and the clear image unite in a satisfying aesthetic in her work, which includes both human evaluation and human judgment, qualities often missing in today's lyric verse. Her work demonstrates an epigrammatic concision and sharp clear outlines one often associates with Celtic art, especially illuminated manuscripts such as the Book of Kells and the Book of Durrow, ridding Welsh poetry of that neo-Romanticism sometimes detectable in the work of Vernon Watkins and Dylan Thomas which produced at times verbiage and an overly aureate style. Bidgood has gone back to the concentrated line of Welsh classical poetry whilst at the same time looking intently at the human drama, 'the fierce element, the fury in our lives' Montale speaks of. These dramas are enacted in poems such as 'Llŵchwr', 'Reading a Landscape', 'Cart Burial, Young Adult Female', and 'Film, "Gwesyn"'. 'That haunting of falling water…the endless fall: / the haunting' of the spirit is captured in 'the concentrated life of [her] irreplaceable solitudes', 'a vision of shining cliffs… a blessing in the light'. Like the interlace and fret of Celtic manuscripts her poetry establishes a continuous chain of connections running from the opening poem all the way through the volume, a wire-and-ribbon effect, as it were, creating a closely-knit spiritual community. Poetry for her is 'the day's gift', but like David Jones she never forgets its roots in the distant Romano-Celtic past:

> For miles the land unfolded
> its flaws, beauties, logic, enigmas,
> contradictions, in unemphatic
> shadowless diversity, like yet unlike a map;
> closer than any map could be
> to those who dug, fenced, coppiced, levelled here,
> bypassed, bridged, laid stone on stone,
> changed and pulled down and built again…

'reading a landscape, / searching for the word "home"'. The elegiac voices of Henry Vaughan and Thomas Traherne can be heard at times in her work, 'the slightest hints and shadows', as well as a more modern poet such as Edward Thomas. She gets right away from bare description (often the bane of contemporary verse) to the human essence of words and life, charting 'the deepest gulf / in an ocean of tears', 'the secret living things', her poetry (over-modestly stated, I think) 'making its little bid to empower / a leap through solstice into light'. The landscapes of Anglesey, Pembrokeshire and Carmarthenshire come to life here: 'the ancient waters roar' and their subterranean power wells up in Bidgood's poetry. Her poems have a tight architectural structure but she manages to maintain simultaneously with that a quality of mature, fluent artistic understatement; they have a quiet distinction to them, an elegant restraint and sensibility which is far removed from the rhetorical excesses, the 'superfluis verbis', of the New Apocalypse school.

Deryn Rees-Jones's pamphlet is also taken up with what she calls 'the subterranean gods', but in her case these are primarily the forces of sex and regeneration, specifically the joys and pains of motherhood. Evanescence also has a strong tug on the poet here: she writes of 'these shortened nights', 'our wintered bones', of being a 'hostage to light, to weather', finding transience embedded in the fossil-record, in the striking image of a trilobite, 'the feathery stone of its cool guitar.' The power of this apprehension is at its clearest in 'Meteor':

> Then the meteor brought us to our feet:
> a stripped atom, trapping electrons
> to excite the darkness with its violet light.
> I remember how it disturbed the heavens,
> burned against the air to leave no trace.

The effect of reading this booklet was to remind me of Byron's stirring lines from Canto XI of *Don Juan*:

> A silent change dissolves the glittering mass.
> Statesmen, chiefs, orators, queens, patriots, kings,
> And dandies, all are gone on the wind's wings.

(The Celtic side of Byron is often forgotten.)

Like Ruth Bidgood, Samantha Wynne-Rhydderch's poems illustrate that 'slow / And patient surgery' R.S. Thomas writes of in 'Iago Prytherch', the hard, clear tone of the verse avoiding unnecessary flourishes. Whether we find her considering buying a dress, working as a waitress, contemplating a suicide, or reviewing her family history, she remains in firm control of her subject, capturing the flow of life, its richness, relationships forming and breaking, in a metre suited to her purpose. She puts the human figure fully back into William Carlos Williams's 'Wheelbarrow' in the poem of that title, rescuing it from mere aesthetic preciousness, and emphasises the opulence of an age compactly in a poem about the sinking of *The Titanic* (with a backward glance at Thomas Hardy's 'The Convergence of the Twain'), 'Oyster Forks: 1000'. Welsh names are lovingly invoked throughout the volume: *Capel Celyn, Storws Wen, Tafarn y Roc*, the words rooted, she says, as 'on a bed of clay.' I like her quiet conversational tone ('You're always nearer to a storm / in an attic') suggestive of proverbs, and her at times subdued eroticism (as in the poem, 'Matador', for instance). Her political stance is less restful, as in 'Welsh Knot' where she writes plangently on the banning of Welsh in nineteenth century schools, an imperialist attempt to poison that rich bed of clay she eulogises. My favourite poems here were 'The Glass Path' and 'Doing Time' where narrative and image coalesce imaginatively. All in all, I thought this a very impressive debut collection.

Peter Finch's poems are very much in the tradition of Tristan Tzara and the Dadaists, with their stress on sound poetry or concrete visualisation, but he widens this vision out to include experiments in macaronic verse, flyting, and Open Field-Projective Verse in the manner of Charles Olson. It is all very entertaining and lively, as in the manner of James Joyce's *Finnegans Wake* – a pell-mell, helter-skelter, topsy-turvy sort of poetry, a collection of what MacDiarmid (in his long poem, *In Memoriam James Joyce*) called 'quashed quotatoes, messes of mottage', a mix-max of English, Welsh and Chinese verses. The title of the volume, *The Welsh Poems*, is a red-herring, a deliberate misnomer, as we are firmly in the country of the mind here, the reader (or listener, possibly) having a strong sense of the maker pulling together disparate (if not at times desperate) things. Finch's poetics reminded me of T. E. Hulme's emphasis on the plasticity of verse, the concentration (as in E. E. Cummings's poetry, for example, or William Burroughs's cut-up prose) on the shape of the verse itself being the syntax, and the alignment of these technical dicta to a Zen Buddhist philosophy stressing the interpenetration of man and inanimate nature (see Finch's poem, 'Zen Cymru', for instance). This is no more weird or wonderful than Joyce's Viconian cycles, Pound's vortices, Yeats's gyres, or Picasso's cubes – it is just one means of approaching tradition and life from an unique angle. The method makes for (in MacDiarmid's phrase) 'wide-angled poems' that incorporate the crazy mosaic of contemporary existence, providing a patchwork grandeur of verbal juxtapositions and incongruities. Experimentalism has all but disappeared from verse, and Finch (as with his colleagues, Bob Cobbing and Chris Torrance) has rightly tried to haul it back in, so that hopefully what the Scots call 'the fouth' of language can be guaranteed and enjoyed in a poetry which possesses the sinuous strength of its own linguistic ferment. In this way, what Edwin Morgan calls 'word-energies' (especially, as in this case, *Welsh* word-energies) can be released in sparking logotechnics without sacrificing a necessary humorous legerdemain, a not entirely serious juggling of responsibilities. Indeed, the free play on scientific themes and models (see 'Quantum Mechanics in the Work of R.S. Thomas' for instance) reminded me at times of Edwin Morgan himself, or of his Glaswegian dialect compatriot, Tom Leonard. The folds and crevices of Welsh history are not ignored in Finch's work. *The Mabinogion*, the poetry of R. S. Thomas and the Methodist hymns of William Pantycelyn are all praised by him in avant-garde terms. The final effect of this book upon me was one which strangely summed up the age: poems of broken words ('daubs', a 'sonic blur', of the lost, of the almost there' the poet calls them, 'verbal fragments, half syllables, seasoned words' which work, he tells us, 'by suggesting, by letting ideas echo'). I was reminded of Dante's Damned, who can only communicate through interrupted utterances: 'There are people under the water. They are sighing. / The surface bubbles and boils with their sighs' (in Basil Bunting's translation, in his 1935 poem, 'The Well of Lycopolis'). They are The Fallen, as we are, and though our language is often risible, it is also, often, very tragic. Finch himself acknowledges this:

Happiness as the pre-supposition of original sin. The happiness in sin, or happiness as the consequence of sin in the particular individual. Happiness as a saving experience by means of faith. Happiness and faith are not the same.

It is too easy not to take experimentalism seriously. Where would we be, for example, without the Imagists, the Vorticists, or the Objectivists? As Edwin Morgan has written (in his 1952 essay, 'Dunbar and the Language of Poetry'):

> Liberty of experiment, importation, invention, and revival were wanted to widen the range of expression and to increase the possibility of those striking original collocations of words where poetry begins to jet out of the melting-pot, with new life whirling in the very materials it springs from.

Language spins its own splendours, like Byron's rainbow that to the shipwrecked men in Canto II of *Don Juan*, 'look'd like hope – / Quite a celestial kaleidoscope.' Or as Aldous Huxley precisely phrased it in 1932: 'It is only by poets that the life of any period can be synthesised' (in *Texts and Pretexts*).

Meirion Jordan is *Agenda*'s chosen Broadsheet poet for this special Welsh issue of the magazine, and *Moonrise* is his first full collection. Several of his poems should be included in later editions of Tony Curtis's anthology of Wales and War. Of eight poems here which take war as their primary theme, there are four of very high quality indeed: 'Poppy field', 'At Srebrenica', 'Dream #7912' and 'Scharnhorst.' The last is so fine I want to quote it in its entirety:

> After the water closed and the smoke dispersed
> they picked the men, white, out of a shivering sea:
> so many voices led off blindfold into the past
> that I can hardly claim to hear. But at night
> I think of the radio operator, still at his set
> as the water rushes round the bulkhead
> into his last message, five fathoms down,
> a sound like scratching, scratching at the door
> that keeps him out, the static: Ich. Ich.

The motif of war is woven into the texture of Jordan's poetry. In a poem about a mosquito whining around his hospital bed, he is reminded of Keith Douglas's war poetry and pays homage to it in a tone similar to Douglas's own praise of Isaac Rosenberg in 'Desert Flowers': 'Douglas I can hear it, the drizzle of wings / from somewhere among these machines...' Social concern is also evident in poems on pit disasters and unemployment, Welsh themes given a new, freshening impetus (see 'A camera at Senghenydd pit' especially, and the title poem, 'Moonrise'). He has a fine feeling for natural description, especially for the sea, and is aware of the richness of the Graeco-Roman tradition (see 'Calculus', 'Circe and Odysseus', 'Head of an athlete in an Ionian shipwreck', 'Ecce homo', 'Einstein on the beach' and 'Dead reckoning'):

> I have been wearing the rhythms of the sea
> all day, the swing of it rising in my arms,

my fingers scathing the backwash
for the solidus of flat stones, raising them
firm as words in my fist

('Solidus' is both an excavated gold coin and a possible evocation of the Roman soldier who dropped it – one is perhaps reminded of Geoffrey Hill's 'the clogged wheel, his gold solidus' in *Mercian Hymns* IV.) These are the opening lines of the volume, and indicate the precision of his poetics. The same credo (if that is not too rigid a term) is evident in other lines such as 'splitting flints down to the last vowel' and in his poem praising Aneirin:

A herdsman tends kine
down a wisp of track, finds

a brooch, iron, its pin broken,
firewood, a warrior floating,

and a torque of gold.

The Celtic inheritance is rich and allied to a fine poetic intelligence. The reader enjoys the roll-call of concatenated Welsh names in 'The new world' and in 'Dyddgu' and is reminded of the early Celtic church and its art (as represented in The Book of Deer, for instance, or in The Lindisfarne Gospels) in phrases like 'coral lizards and the coral snakes', 'an angel in a scoop of rock', 'a tracery where saints appear' 'the gospels of the body', 'The pilgrims gone, / the rain processes like the cadence of a mass', 'a Christ of water and daylight', all of it brought up to date though:

The windowsill carries its bloom
of arc-lights and peroxide flowers
from the hospital that backs on
behind the laurels.

Meirion Jordan's first collection promises much for the future, and he is certainly a Welsh poet to watch.

I have left Andrew McNeillie's book to the last, as I think it the most artistically ambitious, and also because he brings into focus most of the themes looked at above. This is McNeillie's third collection, and although it attempts to balance private concerns with public issues, the latter predominate (though not to the detriment of the former, it must be said). This is no bad thing, not to my mind at least, and indeed where the strength of the volume (and I think it a very powerful volume of poetry) primarily lies. The book opens with the poet meditating on a honeysuckle vine, in a poem with a very strict rhyme scheme, a skill in evidence throughout – 'put your hand to the poem' he says pragmatically later on, and at another point offers the good advice that, 'if you will write poetry, then / observe the disciplines, attend to scansion.' The introductory poem then looks back on the northern European tradition of Ygdrassil (familiar to James Joyce's Stephen Daedalus in his 'ash-plant'), Odin hanging on the World Tree, the vine-clusters of Merovingian sculpture, *The Dream of the Rood,* and to the specifically Welsh vision of Peredur in *The Mabinogion*:

> On the bank of the river
> he saw a tall tree: from
> roots to crown one half was
> aflame and the other green with leaves.

The myth collates pagan solar myths with Christian iconography, a tradition also evident in an early poem of Hugh MacDiarmid's where he celebrates 'A Moment in Eternity', 'Breathing new leaves of life / Upon the eternal air', 'And every leaf a flame'. It is very definitely not the Graeco-Roman grapevine that McNeillie glories in here (though he is not altogether blind to that warm southern legacy, nor to the corruption of Blake's rose with its 'invisible worm, / That flies in the night') but its Celtic counterpart, primarily in its manifestations in Welsh history and politics (but no exclusively so), and the poem signals the book's intentions in that direction:

> So things went until I took
> no care in it, troubling neither to
> pluck it out nor study honeysuckle in a book.
> And so it grew, and slowly grew
> time out of mind and now
> trellis and vine embrace, as if,
> for all the world, for dear life.

Among the poet's tutelary angels are R. S. Thomas (one catches his Calvinist tone at times in lines such as 'The stones on my sill hold their cold'), David Jones, Saunders Lewis (one of the founding members of *Plaid Cymru* and its president from 1926 to 1939), Vernon Watkins (with some reservations), Dylan Thomas and Edward Thomas, the last three elegised in the book. The model of Gerard Manley Hopkins is there in the form of the sequence 'Arkwork', the story of the January 1953 shipwreck of the Stranraer-Larne ferry in which 133 passengers and crew were drowned, which owes a little to *The Wreck of the Deutschland* and to *The Loss of the Eurydice,* and that of Geoffrey Hill's *Mercian Hymns* in the 'Glyn Dŵr Sonnets'. His political hero is Owain Glyn Dŵr, resister of the English, and Eamonn De Valera, Ireland's first President (he recounts an unexpected visit to Wales by the latter organised by the National Union of Teachers in 1950, and his support for Welsh nationalism). He eulogises Welsh poets and painters (such as Iolo Goloch and Carey Morris), the settlers of Patagonia fleeing English imperialism (as before them the Scottish Gaels to Nova Scotia or the Irish to the USA), and rightly berates Matthew Arnold for his hatred of all things Welsh:

> 'The sooner the Welsh language disappears,'
> said St Matthew Arnold, '...the better'
> and he meant every word to the letter.
> Though he rattles on about wheat and tares,
> as if the name of sweetness and light,
> make no mistake: what governs the page
> of this *bien-pensant* Victorian Sage
> is imperialist sweetness and shite.

Arnold's position is even more unforgiveable given that he had written a book entitled *On the Study of Celtic Literature*, published in 1866. (McNeillie's condemnation is rather stronger, to say the least, than that of the Scottish poet John Davidson who, in a posthumously collected essay of 1910, argued that Arnold was merely 'an ineffective apostle of culture'.) I am not convinced, however, by McNeillie's likening of Osama Bin Laden to Glyn Dŵr as a freedom fighter. For one thing, the former is best regarded as a globalist and the latter as a nationalist.

McNeillie intelligently interrogates unique Welsh words like *cynefin* which in its compactness entails an embracing of 'belonging here and now, / in the landscape of your birth and death, /its light and air, and past, at once' (a quality he detects, for instance, in the paintings of Kyffin Williams whose *Waves Breaking Over Reef, Trearddur* of 1994 provides a magnificent cover to the book). Such concision is familiar to us already in the word *hiraeth,* and there is just a hint of a suggestion that G. M. Hopkins knew this word's meaning and significance when he was defining his own aesthetic of 'inscape'. The issue of strife and opposition at the heart of Tony Curtis's two anthologies is also evident here in McNeillie's poetry where he admires the positions of Welsh nationalists from Owain Glyn Dŵr onwards. Like Samantha Wynne-Rhydderch also, he rails against Welsh being forbidden in nineteenth century schools, but he also writes of the forced emigration of Welsh speakers to remote settlements such as Patagonia ('As witness here their Exodus, to save the language and preserve / their heritage and true religion'), and lauds the Celtic likening for bringing 'everything down to earth', and praising the good sense and culture generally of *Y werin*, the people of Wales. He writes of 'war's storm' in his elegy on Edward Thomas, in 'Meditation for Armistice Day', and in the elegy for the painter, Carey Morris. He notes Edward Thomas's prescient foretaste of war, and this reminded me of Alun Lewis's great poem of leave-taking anthologised by Tony Curtis, 'Goodbye':

> I put a final shilling in the gas,
> And watch you slip your dress below your knees...
> You say, 'We paid a guinea for this bed',...

Everything we renounce except ourselves;
Selfishness is the last of all to go...
Yet when all's done you'll keep the emerald
 I placed upon your finger in the street;
And I will keep the patches that you sewed
On my old battledress, my sweet.

Here is an indication of that manly realism Whitley Stokes thought characterised Celtic literature down the ages. McNeillie also has a poem on the burning of Welsh books (including the original Welsh translation of the Bible) by 'Black' Ysgolan in the Tower of London, as a mark of that barbarism which is never quite eradicated from the world. Amongst his favourite books are R. R. Davies's *The Revolt of Owain Glyn Dŵr*, Geoffrey of Monmouth's *Historia Regum Britanniae*, Peter Fallon's translation of Virgil's *The Georgics* (Seamus Heaney has praised the latter's *cynefin*, its 'natural vernacular speech and a general at-homeness on the land' in *The Irish Times*), Thoreau's *Walden*, Mandelstam's *Tristia* (and, by implication, Ovid's work of the same name), and the novels of Bruce Chatwin. The common link here may be the sense of community that is derived from exile and alienation. One great find in this volume is McNeillie's translation of the one poem we know that G. M. Hopkins wrote in Welsh, in *cywydd* form (a form, seemingly, W. H. Auden also liked to play around with), 'Gwalia'. Here are a few lines from it:

    Here thrust of water will
bring faithful witness (man will not),
to our valley's immortal look and lot
and only man's deficiency work ill.

Here as from the hand of god see spring
beauty of goodness, and nourishment
of faith, pure healing bring.

This has a little of the stamp of Hopkins's 'immortal diamond' to it, though I am not at all sure about the lower case 'god.'
    The background to McNeillie's poetry is rooted in that opposition between modernity and the human he writes so eloquently about in his *Times Literary Supplement* review of Alexander Moffat, Alan Riach and Linda MacDonald-Lewis's *Arts of Resistance: Poets, portraits and landscapes of modern Scotland*, arguing the case for the 'resistant value in art' in 'our present age of distraction', 'the depressingly familiar back-story of repression, internecine struggle, clearance, industrialization and consequent rural desolation' created by English imperialism. His poetry gives us in its full glory the 'heart's raised hearth', his 'language his true shield', but recognises at the same time our ingrained mortality:

So in the grains of all success rusts the seed of ruin.
Generations are as dust. Languages no less.

All our 'icons are as dust before the Fates' he says, reminding us that decomposition and corruption belong to the natural order of things. He pitches his words against 'our empty times', knowing that to be an impossible task without the 'haunting shade' of tradition, in this case, the poet's Welsh inheritance. It sometimes happens that a poet's politics will run a little beyond his feelings, but in Andrew McNeillie's case the two sit together well in a balanced relationship, especially in the title poem, 'Slower', a sustained meditation on the Good Friday Agreement. This is certainly a book I think every serous reader of contemporary poetry should buy. Like all true Celtic poets, and like the Irish philosopher George Berkeley, Andrew McNeillie knows that 'things are not just as they seem', and that behind the phantasmagoria lies the pure apprehension of form, 'the story that's as old as time itself' – poetry.

All of these books and pamphlets have one thing in common: they prove, as Rowan Williams has said, writing of R. S. Thomas's work, that 'Poetry is the construction of a more deeply and resourcefully intelligible self which is achieved by pushing the inner tensions of language to the point of new discoveries in form and metaphor.' They also demonstrate that Welsh poetry in English is alive and well, keeping the flames of David Jones and Dylan Thomas lit, though without sacrificing that true inheritance which has its roots in the culture which produced *The Mabinogion* and the elegies of those two great court-singers, Taliesin and Aneirin. As Czeslaw Milosz has said, 'The vital tasks have to be taken over by the peripheries, by less illustrious nations, simply because the others have grown slack', and commenting on these words the Scottish critic, Cairns Craig, has written: 'Recognising the vitality of the periphery is the first step towards overthrowing the dominant conceptions of tradition; overthrowing those traditions will release the vitality of the periphery.' That energy is evidenced in each of the works reviewed here, demonstrating that continuing strength and high quality we expect of a great tradition.

Gwyneth Lewis

Lundy

Stile

First rule on boats: never stand
one leg on the vessel, the other on land.

You know what might happen: undignified splits,
then splashings. If you must be betwixt

and between, be careful. This is how Lleu
was slain by Blodeuwedd, who betrayed

his secret. Immortal, he could only be killed
with a lance forged on Sundays by highly skilled

blacksmith. And if he were caught
in limbo, perched with one foot

on a billy goat's back, one on a trough,
balancing tipsily, Close enough

to me perched on this wobbly stile.
They say I should choose. But I'll

sit here longer, till the Half-Way Wall
bucks like a bronco. And I won't fall

till I see sun blaze on that thrown spear
made only for me, which I'm told I should fear.

Fog

Above all else fog shuns
        publicity,
wants intimate islands,
        private seas
(collisions don't matter).
        It has a selective memory:

A lonely fog horn
        cries to mate
with answering sirens
        (too late, too late!).
An island is
        a rooted boat

and granite vessels
        do set sail
through seas of fog
        towards the wail
of mainland lights
        three ponies stand
at the Half-Way Wall,

dew in their coats.
        Yarrow's furred
with moisture. We are blind,
        steering by what's heard
through white-out. The voyage
        is inwards, towards words.

iii

Map

The heart's an island half a mile
by three. I'm its cartographer
and sex promontories.

See the dartboard heli pad?
We scored a bull's eye on that day
we eloped from the mainland.

Our scenic look-out. I would like a plaque
with my name on for loving
seals and bladderwrack,
sea gnawing the same old chewing gum of rocks.

You are the measuring rod
to my theodolite. When my time comes
I'll map this entrance to the Underworld.
Come with me. We can chart the route
together, onwards and on to the last known field.

iv

Appointment

'Doctor,
I have an island inside my eye,
a floater.'
'You're sure to arrive before you die.'

'Doctor,
I have an island on the brain,
but it keeps on moving.'
'Take these pills for a week,
then come back again.'

'Doctor,
I see and island in my dreams.'
"My nights are swept by the lighthouse beams
of traffic. Leave a specimen.'

'Doctor,
I've found the island of my soul!
Mermaids swim there beside the seals...'
'This is a property for sale.
You have no income, man.
Get real.'

'Doctor,
I have an island inside my heart.'
'An island is a heart.'
'I need to go there!'
'Leave yourself behind.'

'Doctor,
I have nowhere to go. It's over!'
'At last you're talking sense!
Now take this compass, I'll bring a chart,
this ECG will do. There's an art
to finding an island. The tides
in the breath are treacherous.
We'll go together.
It's not very far...'

(Commissioned by BBC Radio 4)

153

Pascale Petit

Roots (The Pedregal)

Look! I'm lying here serene for once,
no parents on the horizon,
just rocks and gashes –

just one continental plate
sliding over another
like the very first couple.

If I'm wearing my orange dress
it's because I'm the sparks
between them.

I fizzed out of my stone mother
and broke her. The jolts
still rock me.

She fed me lava,
so I bonded
with this hard ground.

Peering down a crack,
I whisper 'Pedregal'
and she echoes back.

It's enough for me to live on today,
this aftershock of a voice
that punches a hole

through my chest
where I should have a heart.
But look at this lush plant

I've coaxed from my marrow,
this love-vine
with my blood for sap,

which winds its leaves around me
as if I'm the sun
crashed out of the sky.

Suckle

In my white baby smock
I'm pristine as a glacier.

There's a smell of ozone
and blue milk. A face

rears above me, covered
by an Olmec mask.

I paint to conjure my nurse –
her breasts like lily beds,

the tip of my brush touching
my tiny head as it ages

overnight. The pigment crackles
on the palette – I work

at the velocity of light.
Behind me, an ivory glass leaf

will shatter if I stop.
The sky pours

shooting stars of tears –
how quickly my eyes lose their fire.

My ear opens its canal
to listen for the hunger-cry

perched like an insect
on swamp water, the trembling

rings of earth's throat –
when I finish those baby lips

so they can suckle.

Tiffany Atkinson

00.52

after Catullus's poem 52

Give it up, Catulla! Take the sea for its
easy amnesia; the car, its intimate
monoxides - why hang about? Your work could be
done by a monkey;

no family to speak of; and most friends would
be elsewhere - networking, accepting prizes,
dropping off the kids, out shopping, getting laid.
Consider the blade

in the boutique-scented bathroom, gentle drifts
of Paracetamol, the empty bottles
at a photogenic angle, all your small
affairs in order;

back, back to the still, white centre, quiet as
a pill. It's just an exercise in self-will.
You might do worse than think about it, lady:
all you could let go.

Aurelius

after Catullus's poem 21

handsomely preaches non-attachment.
Catulla grows smooth as a pebble,
as an old spoon, as a grey Jag E-type,
as a new hand. One elastic band

tight on her left wrist, to remind her:
take less. Ask for less. Desire's like
hair: the quotidian, impossible fixation.
She has left her hair. She finds she's

grown quite thin; has always *wanted*
to be thin. A paradox? Aurelius says
a woman has no business doing logic.
Until then she'd let him win at chess.

And Rufus's youngest, ASBO-boy,
whose hot-wire skills are known through
seven counties, leads the after-school-club's
weekly Meditation On The Pure Heart!

Mentorship, they call it. Leave him well
alone, you gaylord English kiddy-fiddler,
was how Rufus put it to him outside
Dempsey's. So she heard. And just like

that, was freshly smitten with his total,
solar inability to give a shit. You know,
the stylist said, while touching up her roots,
that your hair grows even when you're dead.

After Bluebeard

two years after, she can stride
through almost all the castle's corridors
and is fine. Fine. No-one can
recall such frequent hunting parties,

springtime festivals and healing-fields.
Her sister climbs the tower
as the waste-ground clears itself—
the ratty polythene and slashed tyres

peeling back on rich lawns, perfect
for the summer's reading circles. She
has opened all the rooms and smelted
every key but one; and this a meditation

on the stain that runs clear through her
like the letters through a stick of rock.
She can't bring herself to ask just what
it is about her that unlocks another's

horror-chamber. There was his blade
at the strop of her throat, the unexpected
breeze of French cologne. His weight.
And once again, she's pushed out wings

and drifted up. Her crown nuzzles
the ceiling. Now the whole outrageous
kingdom must dissolve. It's like…
It's like… But that is the business

of dreams. She's on the beach;
bare feet, a borrowed wedding-gown,
grains of sand beneath her fingernails.
All fears, all pebbles, have their inner,

secret names. Her brothers,
leaning on the sunset, sow the sea
with skimming-stones. Look, husband.
The astonishing impartiality of light.

Zoë Brigley

Her Last Rochester

She's in the attic room in a Georgian house
in the town that you knew but never liked.
She waits for a bridegroom to arrive home
when he will play the double bass
stretching the gentle bow across the strings
as rain gathers in islands on the slanted windows.

What did you wear, that last time she saw you?
The mole-skin coat bought together.
In her dreams, it flaps like a crow's wings
beside the bead of your empty crow eye.
She's writing after so long, sensible or not.
She's not asking for anything, not ever.

You're probably on your way somewhere,
about to catch a bus or a train, smelling of soap
and holding a tattered rucksack. Or maybe
you're only boiling peas in the kitchen,
imagining the saucepan as a big top
silver-lidded over the performers.

She remembers how sitting on the beaten up sofa,
you said, 'I'll have you for my own',
and she believed you. Or there was the time
off Taksim Square when you last punched her,
your fist in her stomach and afterwards
you both made your way to the hotel in silence.

She hadn't thought of you for a while
until a friend of yours phoned and told her this:
that you were travelling again, Hong Kong or China,
that you had found someone else and
that this other woman was at last
the second person in your life that you'd loved.

And she wanted to ask if the first person was her
or if it ever figured at all? Her last Rochester,
I wanted to tell you that there isn't a day
that goes by that she doesn't think of you,
and yet for all that, it was never you at all.
It was never you that she wanted.

The Scent Bottle

'the vessel in which she had sent my box, being stranded on the coast of Devonshire, in consequence of which the box was dashed to pieces with the violence of the sea & all my little property, with the exception of a very few articles, swallowed up in the mighty deep'.
                    Maria Branwell in a letter to her future husband, Patrick Brontë

I am a long time coming but when I do arrive,
I sit by the mirror, my stopper protruding
a severed stalk, a silver eye, a squat key.

She sits before me waiting for something
and cradles the shock of my cold body in her palm.
I am hardly beautiful and long lost my newness

– blasted by salt and scratched by sailors –
and yet, in the deep heady scent of me
is something else: a voyage by ship that skims

the North Sea and rounds the coast for Penzance
to the blink of a teasing lighthouse,
the long beckoning of a weathered stone pier,

the slap of pilchards on the cobbles, and rowing boats
dwarfed by larger vessels: the Amity and Fame,
the Grace, the One and All, the Happy Return.

In my perfume is not a walled garden,
but the watery stench of the tide-waiter and mariner,
the pasteboard smell of printers and bookbinders,

the sickly malsters on Market Jew Street
and the burnt liquorice of the tanners and saddlers,
the tang of the physician's, the caramel of boot-makers,

the foggy wool of the tailors and drapers,
that peruke maker's flowery chamber
and honeyed fat of the tallow-chandler,

dust grasping in the deepening shaft of Wherry Mine
and smelted tin rasping metallic like blood on the tongue,
until the stopper fits me again and that other place sets sail.

We wait together, her and I, and beyond the garden,
the purple moor spreads out before us
like a rough and mothering ocean and she stumbles

out into the heather catching another scent on the wind.

The Hair Bracelet

(the bracelet belonging to Charlotte Bronte)

After it was plaited so that each tiny thread
wound this way and that to bind the band
together, I took my bangle of tawny hair
to the jewellers where the intricate weave
of the hair bracelet was fitted with a golden clasp
and a stone, the colour of yew berries.
Nothing could match the twine
of my golden armlet, except perhaps
after I died, when the severed curls,
of my sisters and I, wound their way
to each other in their funeral envelopes.

The Dispensary

In a hotel room that was once
the dispensary of the Brontës' doctor
and with our marriage still a year away,
I think of the first time that we came here,
walking the steepness
of Haworth's hill, climbing but never quite
reaching the Withens. From the bed
in this small hotel room, my gaze passes
through the window to float over Haworth:
the sheer mill chimney, the stark whiteness
of a wind turbine that tenses its blades
against the gale. Lying on the hotel bed,
I recall a morning outside Haworth Church
when the trees, that never existed
in the Brontës' time, made an aisle
for me to walk and the leaves trembled
like the whisper of a promise and I felt them
like the hands of a very first lover.

Zoë Skoulding

Gwydyr Forest

through white trees nothing said
      the edges grow sharper the hills
            farther away with each degree

below freezing under feathered
      water landscapes turn to vapour
            in our mouths clouding the route

you test the surface by stamping this weight of
      our bodies enough to live by measure
            an echo from one side of the lake to

another in summer there are dragonflies
      now heat is something I can't even
            remember we call back to our

outlines scuttle stones across the water
      stacked in lattices of molecules we
            reassemble contact held to breaking

I can do more dangerous things
      just with my eyes or crack the ground
            without even trying we fall

over moss tundra scale shrinks
      to skin print claw track in ice
            that up to this point holds

The museum for disappearing sounds

exhibit 1

the voice lost in reconstructions of itself
trails off at the end of a cable
leaks into empty rooms
implicated more and more by every word
I am translated into wires
lose this gain that become

exhibit 2

in breath a crackle of static
disturbance
            a detuned radio in one lung

drones erase one other
            electricity sings in D
tyres slur across the street

a shoreline just out of sight
            at the base of the skull

you hold the rise
and decay in its arc
            before dispersal
in wind on the microphone

cough in wave forms
count the layers

but when the light goes quiet
you sleep under air
            roaring
through the tunnel of your throat

exhibit 3

today I'm dripping into forests
           far into sleep
where you can't find me
cannot catalogue the rustle of larch
unpick
        pixel by pixel
the stones under my feet

exhibit 4

in thin vibrations of the phone
a voice shimmers on the end of a line

while outside
           ring dove calls
slip over branches into memory

breath hops and starts
        is this is this is this is this is this
I vanish in lossy compression

birds listen
           come in and drop out

the rhythms that cradle us
turn to an I-you stammer of ringtones
on the nervous system's high whine

exhibit 5

in a frame of silence
          the spectrum
       shivers into transmission

in a forest of black and white
          off-channel   branches
interlace over water   dark
     and interrupted light

the moon is close closer
or retreating
behind the traffic far off

     coming and going
accelerates to slow-mo as rhythm
turns to pitch and sinks to drone

Jeni Williams

On Travelling and Maps

it was, possibly, a mistake –
to travel so far, so fast –
although it remained an adventure,
it was on shaky foundations.

Yet he knew how to read maps, to admire clarity,
to seek only the distance between things; knew
how to forget the nervous intravenous insertion,
by razor or needle, of fire, to ignore
the churning rattle and whisper of the forest floor,
and the black insects, everywhere hysterical with dusk.

For how else to travel from one place to another?
How else to leave both behind?

As he drove, solid land slid into swamp,
abandoned histories resurrected themselves
in flashes on the glittering edges of vision.
His bloody thoughts surfaced to minefields.

He stumbled further, through dripping water and a nightfall of spiders
But his sense of gratitude for north and west
drew him onward through a partial paper world.
The words faded before they turned familiar.

In the bone-thin mountains he listened to the echo of his thoughts,
white paper slipping through rigid fingers.
He was tired, aching, bitten.
Yet, wet amongst the clouds,
he forgave the shortcomings of maps,
stared at the purple sky, at the starflowers opening in early morning frost
The ice catching in his throat.
The birds stirred and sang Bartók.

Time Passes

'Music...breathing of statues'
(Rilke)

The passing of time is a heartbeat, is
dust on the sideboard, thickening, a drift
of moments, the accumulation of
inheritances: a chair, a table,
a picture, a lamp.
                    The hard dark wood lasts,
gleaming with the years' ponderous weight,
monumental in a room that softens
fades with the dull, the slow fading eye.

But, heart beating, listen to the bright sound:
music holding back inharmonious time.
The frozen moment floats,
frozen light over the dark furniture,
a clean white space.

                    Deny the soft decay.
The unattainable moment, stillness,
a locked heartbeat, shivers into being
in a moment, hangs only a moment.

Voice soars, piano diminuendo:
the fine order of furniture falters.
How bright that music, built against decay.
Brightness like snow powders my chilling breast,
settles. Feel the cold settle blissfully.

Listen. It will last.
It is time holding its breath,
It is a moment, carved, breathing.

Two Chosen Young Broadsheet Poets

Angela Lewis and Meirion Jordan

Angela Lewis is 24 years old. She is Welsh on her father's side and she lives in Cardiff, having recently completed an MA in Early Celtic Studies at Cardiff University. She has won several awards for her poetry, most recently the inaugural Robin Reeves Prize in 2008. Her poems have appeared in journals including *Modern Poetry in Translation, New Welsh Review* and *Poetry Wales,* and she is the recipient of a 2008 – 2009 New Writer's Bursary from Academi.

Arawn's Wife

Suddenly, the nights have changed shape.
The first is long and narrow.
Arawn's wife lies on her side,
stares at the back of her husband's head,
follows the spool of his breath.
An hour passes before she sleeps.

Weeks. The nights tighten:
she kicks at her husband's legs,
stammers his back with her hands,
asks his shoulders again and again
why he has changed.
He ignores her; she cries; her days
are stiff with tiredness. She is taut
with her maids, suspects each in turn.

Months, and the nights draw back.
Moonlight is usual now,
soothes her, like distant music.
She trails the curve of his neck
with quiet fingers.
She cries a little, still,
her body weighed down
with useless organs, with such
pointless and bulky cushions of flesh.

The third season slows to the fourth
and the nights are shallower,
like young waves in a retreating tide.
He tells her his dreams in the
mornings; she tells him hers.

Teyrnon's Wife

If you are lying, I can't tell.
You sleep deeply, eat heftily;
each pocket of your body still
clasps its old scent.
                        In privacy,
your fingers drawl my back,
their pace and pressure unchanged –
and your lips buffing my shoulder,
the rough of your knee parting mine:
all as it should be.

But I watch the child mimicking
you in the field; the narrow window,
the sun sweeping back. His shadow
shakes into yours, keeps to its line.
That night, when you knocked at
my room – 'I have found a boy,
if you will keep him' –

something came loose in me.
Now, you say, you have an idea
of his mother: the Lady who waits
by the horse-block at her husband's gate,
and carries strangers to court, in penance
for losing their child.

You don't invite me there with you.
I would have ridden her, the mare,
and spurred her for good measure;

only, I never want to know
the saddle of her hips under mine,
the charge of her breasts against my hands.

Manawydan

I have worn her down:
I mused for hours on outsoles and uppers,
pondered over this leather or that –

I made her test the tread of my shoes,
chased and counted her footsteps, and now
I don't know where she walks; my stitches won't hold.

It hurts to think of the flex of her feet as she moves:
the arches hitching and flattening,
the flicker of those birch-bones, like shadows under the skin.

I have heard that in some fantastic, faraway land,
they break and fold the feet of small girls
and bind them in silk,
making their women exquisite, and lame;

and I dream of Rhiannon,
bandaged and bloodied, and twisting
on a strange forest floor, as cherry blossom falls
and gathers in drifts, like red snow.

Llwyd's Wife

For weeks, I have worried
that you will be born a timid,
snuffling thing, fraught with dreams

of wheat fields high as forests,
of giants looming towards you
with gaping hands.

You drift at the end of my blood:
every picture, each word,
taps like a code down this cord

to you poised,
wide-eyed in the dark as a sentry
and ready; receiving, receiving.

Aranrhod

One comes with the other;
you may call either one by each name.
Wolf: boar. One held down the girl
while the other held shut the door.

Boar: stag. I left both of my brothers,
but one followed me to my castle's gate.
Uncle: father. He holds up the child
as a priest lifts bread and wine.

Son: nephew. I do not recognise him.
A gawping boy, vacant
as a flower's splayed face.

Goewin

He has made his peace with my husband.
They embrace in our hallway,
and I sit with them both at table.

He is here for a favour: a bride for his son,
and the men select oak flower, meadowsweet, broom.
They take turns to pluck, thread and twist
until their hands slide with juices,

until, at last light,
they coax a girl from carpels and stamens,
from sepals and slender petals.

She stands naked between them,
skin sticky with sap,
breasts still swelling from her chest.
Their tips slowly firm and ripen, dark as fumitory.

Notes:

This sequence gives voice to often-overlooked characters from the *Mabinogion*, the principal collection of Medieval Welsh prose:

Arawn's Wife

Without telling his wife, Arawn trades place and form with another man, Pwyll.

Teyrnon's Wife

Teyrnon finds and raises an abandoned child, probably the missing son of Pwyll and his wife, at whose court Teyrnon once served.

Manawydan

Manawydan takes work as a shoemaker. His wife, Rhiannon, vanishes.

Llwyd's Wife

Llwyd's pregnant wife is turned into a mouse. She is captured, and narrowly survives.

Aranrhod

Aranrhod refuses to acknowledge her illegitimate son, who was raised by her brother Gwydion. Gwydion and his brother were, previously, turned into animals as punishment for rape.

Goewin

Goewin's husband forgives his friend Gwydion for Goewin's rape.

Meirion Jordan, 23, was born near Swansea in South Wales in 1985. He studied mathematics at Somerville College, Oxford, and has just completed an MA in Creative Writing at UEA, Norwich. His first collection of poems, *Moonrise*, is published by Seren and is reviewed here in W S Milne's Omnium Gatherum of Welsh books..

Cat, Cé and Fidach

> *Tonight I am lord of the isles.*
> *I have dug at Finlaggan and Dunadd*
>   *for the ancient sky*
> I carry it over my head for a tent.
> I have taken the chapel stones
>   for bread.
>   *I have measured the tide-mark*
>   *by the arms of the high cross*
> The waves
>   sweep stars
>   from either shore.
>   *The prow*
>   *sheds rosaries*
>   *to the herons*

> The houses are open in the dark
>   the table is laid
>   *the table is ready*
>   sit with us
>   sit with us
>   eat

Calchfynedd

as though the dead know
the instrument
of their impression

dust-maned and crowned
with dust I wait
pitted with dust

on the claws that flenced
on high days
before the feast

in the dark eyes, and the noise
of the horsemen
and of the wheels, and the chariots

– like all those
of a toothless race
I lapse into quotation

Man of sorrows

(Brittany 1940)

Fearful   between two shores
one granite   pilgrim-shouldered
the other   merciful   appointed
        and hung with storms.

Foundered at last   without searchlights
        over the questing sea:
rock-armours   rumours;
                        the day's articles drove them
                                from his thought.

        Clouds
                light's ladders
                                the scarce nails of flame
they pierced his log-book.   The radio
whittled his bones away.   In the last
        he was only   a name   a lightness
                a shadow of cloth: his ships
a haul of rust   creasing the tide.

The small animals (from The Robots)

Forever and forever the small animals.
The landscape of lizards and toads
in the dry bowls of hills cold as sunset settles
on the stones.

Forever and forever the small towns,
and the smaller kingdoms: the dominion
of a two-acre field, and the dust settling
behind a wood plough:

and the life in miniature, however hard,
however far into the margins, breaking soil
between hovels, the concrete hollows
in the great aftermath

which we must be living: Turing's invisible
Manchester, the Dartmouth conference;
they under the long shadows of the bombs,
the black-and-white people

goofing into the lens, a semicircle of chairs
and smiles. Then twilight for a quarter century
to return as scene-shifters for the drama,
mainstream computing.

Forever and forever the bold tomorrows
of yesterday, where Buck Rogers takes flight
over desertscape, or the future of workaday
velures and lycras;

the home of the flying car, the ray-gun,
the home atomic power plant, and the sun
of California backlots raining down on you,
punter, forever.

Forever and forever the cockroaches,
and the rats and rattlesnakes, the jackrabbit
and the spider, the small embodiments
of a wider mercy

which extends into the rapidly-indexing
now, as we strain to see the small worlds
surface from the molecules of their birth
forever.

Notes for Broadsheet Poets

Patricia McCarthy interviews Gillian Clarke

P McC: *When did you first become interested in poetry and when and why did you start writing it? Or should I simply quote the wonderful first poem, 'First Words' of your new collection, which seems to answer my question!*

G Clarke: I loved nursery rhymes and songs from earliest childhood, then playground games and chants, the morning hymn at school with lines like 'there is a green hill far away'. Even the times table's lovely litany chanted in class gave me a thrill. Also, the sound of Welsh and English in a house of talk. They say that I made up rhymes as soon as I could speak, and poems and stories as soon as I could write.

P McC: *Who are the poets you most admire?*

G Clarke: Shakespeare, John Donne, Keats, all the dead men I studied at school and university. Later, Emily Dickinson, Yeats, R.S. Thomas, Ted Hughes, the marvellous 14th century Welsh poet Dafydd ap Gwilym. Then my contemporaries, Seamus Heaney of course, and a host of younger poets, so many of them women.

P McC: *Your fine career as a poet covers a wide span. What was it like when you first started out, especially as a woman poet?*

G Clarke: The word 'career' sounds odd, because any success there was came poem by poem. There was a time when, at the age of 30, with three small children and my degree and dreams of being a writer a distant memory, I thought my so-called career was down the drain. I wrote in notebooks, kept a journal, but never typed or submitted poems anywhere. Then a few poems were sent – not by me – to *Poetry Wales*, and were accepted. One was called 'The Sundial'. That first 'yes' was very important, as it is to all writers. In my education poets were not women, were not Welsh, were not alive. When my first poems appeared in magazines, the world of London publishing was an exclusive one. For example, the *TLS* reviewed no books from small Welsh publishers, or small publishers anywhere I suppose. In Wales in the '60s all visible poets were male. At my very first reading in the '70s, alongside two distinguished Welsh writers, one told me that the other had sneered at 'women' on the stage. I had, apparently, been better received than he had. That attitude has long been swept away.

P McC: *Do you think there should be any distinctions made between male and female poets? Kathleen Raine, Blakean scholar and poet, let down her own sex, in a way, by asserting that 'women can't write poetry'. Virginia Woolf, in her essay,*

'A Room of One's Own', asked why, for example, there has never been a female Shakespeare, and suggested that this will only happen when women start to write androgynously. How do you react to these two statements?

G Clarke: Each poet is unique, each one has a distinct voice. All that we are, our culture, gender, life experience is in our art. You can't 'make' these distinctions. As a poet I feel a lot closer to, say, Seamus Heaney than to Kathleen Raine, with whose writings, including the remark you quote, I have little in common. As for Virginia Woolf's question, there has been no second male Shakespeare either. There may, however, have been a Virginia Woolf, a female Dafydd ap Gwilym, a Donne, a Keats, and many another woman of letters unseen and unheard. It is history's great silence and our loss. Some may yet be discovered, but most are voices lost forever. I find that thought very moving.

P McC: *I notice that you are a tutor on the M Phil in Creative Writing at the University of Glamorgan and that you are President of the Writers' Centre you founded in North Wales in 1990. Presumably Creative Writing Schools at universities in the UK didn't exist when you were young. What do you think of them? Do you think that poetry can be taught? Would you advise a budding young poet to enrol in one?*

G Clarke: This is a complicated question. The art of poetry cannot be taught, but natural talent can be recognised and nurtured. First, the M Phil at Glamorgan: it is, as far as I know, like no other. All the tutors are published writers, and we individually agree to work with an applicant who is already committed to writing a book: a collection of poems, short stories or a novel. Each year I take only one new poet, whose potential and commitment shine out of the first submitted poems. The poet writes. I encourage, talk poetry, get tough, raise the game. We meet four times, and the rest is by e-mail. Second, Ty Newydd, the equivalent of the Arvon Foundation in England and Scotland, has a different purpose. Fine poets do sometimes arrive out of the blue – I first met the young, unpublished Kathleen Jamie, and Alice Oswald, while tutoring Arvon courses – but the five-day courses have a wider purpose. They are open to all, and do not claim to teach people to write. The workshops prompt new writing, creative discussion and the exchange of ideas. Reading, talking, listening, lively discussion, sharing a love of words, making friendships over a text, and having 'permission' to indulge in time to write away from home, are as important as the tutoring. Finally, I think a budding poet should take every chance to attend readings, and attend a Ty Newydd or Arvon course. There a new poet finds a sympathetic home, and, if the work is ready, some good tips, after which an editor might consider a small pile of poems. I'd prefer a budding poet to study anything but creative writing at BA level. Get educated first!

P McC: *What words of advice, from your experience, would you give to a young poet? E.g. How do you get going on a poem, do you make many drafts, what about the form (or free expression)?*

G Clarke: First, read, read, read, and write every day, maybe keep a journal, or a notebook. I'll pass on advice I heard from two great poets: R.S.Thomas: 'Read something substantial, then take pen and paper to see what words will do.' Ted Hughes: 'Throw nothing away. Put it in a drawer. When you look at it later it may catch fire.' I usually do three or four pages of drafts before I'm satisfied with a poem, leaving the first scribble alone long enough for it to become a stranger. Overnight is usually enough for you and the poem to reconsider. Never write yourself to exhaustion, or the poem will be exhausted too. A poet needs energy, an excitement for language, and a compulsion to write.

P McC: *What are your pet hates in poetry?*

G Clarke: It's a matter of taste, and I would not belittle any contribution to the world of rhythm and rhyme. Great mountain ranges need foothills. However, I hate puns – boys' toys, I think! – too many adjectives, pomposity, and last lines that flag up the 'Meaning'. But it is easier to say what I love: for me a poem is a rhythmic way of thinking, and all true poetry must have cadence, clarity, with further layers to unwrap after the first reading, and at least one line or phrase that stops the heart and stays in the mind.

P McC: *Do you discipline yourself to write every day, or do you write poetry only when you are inspired?*

G Clarke: I have always kept a journal. I love a fine black pen, a little black Daler-Rowney notebook with acid free paper, and some weather and a view outside the window to get me started. Inspiration is lovely – to be suddenly startled by a kind of passion. However, it is perfectly possible to write a poem on purpose, and sometimes the purposeful poem can be as good as those that just come from the air. They can surprise, can catch fire. You can put yourself in the way of 'inspiration', research the subject, and find that a new lexicon awaits you in a new subject.

P McC: *Your Welshness – how has this influenced your poetry? You do use words in Welsh and phrases between the English in your poems, but do you ever write a whole poem in the Welsh language? In the poem 'Letting the Light In' in your new collection, there is a very vivid image of 'The et cetera of terraces / like paragraphs of longhand / in the old language'. This reminds me of Seamus Heaney's comparison of hedges to scribble. This 'old language', though, 'a line of verse in Welsh from the Age / of Poets', which you elaborate on in the poem 'Welsh Gold' from the same collection, presumably harks back to the Bardic tradition and to Taliesin. How steeped are you in this? What is your attitude also to Welsh mythology which you incorporate into your poetry at times?*

G Clarke: Wales is a bilingual country, with more Welsh in some areas, and in some families, than others. It's where I have always lived, it's my country, my background, my culture, and I know no other. Welsh is often called 'the old language', (known also as 'British', once the first language of almost the whole of Britain) but it is still spoken and written and was the first language of both my parents. Unfortunately my mother insisted on her daughters speaking only English. Welsh was the familiar language – my father always spoke it to his mother, who lived with us. But stories, rhymes, books and education were in English. Where I use Welsh in a poem it is because the Welsh word seems right. In 'Welsh Gold' the line you quote suggests a vein of gold like a line on an old manuscript, and it does, in that case, refer to the bardic tradition, and to Taliesin and Aneurin. Where I live now I hear Welsh every day. I have acquired Welsh as an adult, read and translate Welsh, and sometimes a Welsh word seems more natural than its English equivalent. Mythology was part of my story-world from the very start. My father placed the stories of the Mabinogion in the topography we inhabited, as if Bendigeidfran had set out that very morning to tow his fleet across the Irish Sea. I believed every word, and still do.

P McC: *You are obviously fascinated by language, 'stirred by song and story' ('A Recipe for Water'), and still, in your latest collection, 'wanting the words fresh' ('Library Chair'). In fact, the whole corpus of your poetry could be said to represent a study of language with its names, its litanies, its sounds, its images, its music. As you say in the new poem, 'The Accompanist', 'So the poem speaks / from the silence of the page'. Do you feel the language, or the singing, in your own poetry has evolved over the years? Has there perhaps been a shift from the more personal to the impersonal and, if so, has this been deliberate?*

G Clarke: Yes, I love language. It is the prime mover in my compulsion to write. It is difficult to speak of change in one's own work - I hope I still have the voice in which I wrote my first published poems. However, I think poets get better with practice, experience, reading and hearing other voices. As for a shift of subject, this is no doubt to do with living in a wider world than I did when I began to write, forty years ago in a house full of children. I travel now, and live in two places.

P McC: *Relating to the above, music of composers, of instruments and especially of garden birds that 'ring like a tambourine' such as the blackbird seems to be woven, like polyphonic strands, into your own poetic music. Can you explain in greater detail your love of music?*

G Clarke: This question takes me by surprise. Certainly I love sound, especially birdsong. Perhaps because my two sons are musicians, and my husband's ear for music is exceptionally alert, they allow me to be the family wordsmith, and I leave musical ability and taste to them. I hate background music and prefer silence or the ordinary sounds of daily life while writing: voices, birdsong, a tractor working in the field over the hedge. However, sometimes at a live concert, or hearing the wind sing in a gate, I can be overwhelmed and all words are lost. I write radio plays, and dream of writing a play for radio with no words, only sounds. Well! Maybe just a few words!

P McC: *You write a lot about the rural life, and especially about sheep. Your moving sequence 'Making the Beds for the Dead' in the collection of that name about the foot and mouth virus in 2001 shows that you are still, as an adult, an integral part of that life, no outsider. This makes a change from poets such as Heaney, Montague, who use their childhood memories of being brought up on small Irish farms, but no longer live that rural life.*

G Clarke: My experience of the rural versus the city differs from Heaney's and Montague's. Their lives divided a rural childhood from a sophisticated, urban adulthood. My two lives ran concurrently. I was born and raised in and around Cardiff and brought up my children there, but spent my childhood reading about children running wild in the countryside, and all holidays 'at home' on my paternal and maternal grandparents' farms in north and west Wales. Thus I postponed my total commitment to the countryside until middle age. As the children left home, I gradually shifted my life west to a small long-house in Ceredigion we had owned since the '70s. Heaney was raised on a farm. I wasn't. In my childhood we 'went home' on holiday to Pembrokeshire, and as a young child I was dispatched to the heaven of my grandmother's farm by the sea to escape the bombs. For this reason I have always had inside me both the country and the city. I wrote 'Making the Beds for the Dead' in reaction to something that is uniquely British within Europe: the dichotomy between the country and the city. I wanted to tell the story of the bad handling of a terrible episode in our history. The situation was far better managed in Wales, where even in Cardiff most Welsh people have a link with the north and west of Wales, and the countryside remains a part of people's family history. My new book, *A Recipe for Water*, has much more of the city in it. There is another reason for the difference you mention: famous male poets are weaned from the life of their roots by academic life and prestigious university posts. Women with children must usually stay at home. I have never had a full-time job. I could not take a fellowship away from my children's home and school until they grew up, when I accepted the post of poet-in-residence at Lampeter, 15 miles from Blaen Cwrt, then our ruinous cottage, now our habitable home. We have a pad in Cardiff now too. I need the city and the country.

P McC: *Linking to the previous question, I notice the 'city' features, like a person, in* A Recipe for Water. *I also notice that the modern life with its headphones, computers etc. is creeping more and more into your poetry. You write a very witty poem, 'A T-Mail to Keats', saying that poets never die, for 'The old poetry drums in the living tongue'.*

G Clarke: The city sequence began when I was Capital poet for Cardiff in 2005-6, the city's centenary year. It evolved as a radio play. The City was the narrator in the drama. I love radio drama because it has the potential to be poetry. You can do anything on radio because the listener is your collaborator. It leaves space for the listener's imagination, as poetry does. As for headphones and computers: I'm the daughter of a BBC radio engineer, and have always loved the latest gadgets of communication: computers, mobile phones, dongles and digital radios. I had one of the first mobile phones, a car-phone, a monstrous box with a curly wire, kept in the car boot and plugged in when needed. I owned an early Amstrad, and used its language in a poem about the legendary Olwen, who left her white footprints where she walked. And yes, I long for science to untangle string theory and crack the mystery of time, so that we can send T-mails to dead poets, just as they still send their lovely lines across the centuries to us.

P McC: There is a lovely balance, in your poetry, with your 'quicksilver tongue', between the elegiac and the celebratory. What special powers do you think poetry has in our present age?

G Clarke: I have said elsewhere that a poem needs just one howl or halleluiah. I like to think that poetry can still catch the heart. What we call poetry first arose from spells and chants. The Bards had jobs as genealogists, remembrancers, and elegy and celebration held the tribe together. Poetry is natural. It's like song. People love rhythm and rhyme, are moved by language. They just need to be receptive and to listen in the right circumstances. You should hear the roars of approval a thousand teenagers make at Poetry Live, for example. If message and sound sing and the audience is open-hearted, it works. I just wish it could reach everyone.

Kites

A gilded initial. A pair. Four
following the combine over the barley,
a flaunt of raptors flexing tail and wings.
Flamboyance. Flames on air.

Sky and field are an open book
of land and light, flux and flair,
of air uttering the updraughts
and slipstreams of inflexion,

of flesh-hungry angels cleaning the field
after harvest, eyes arrowing earth
for the crushed and the bloody,
for the stopped heart.

Peter Carpenter interviews Zoë Brigley

Zoë Brigley was born in 1981 and was brought up in Caerphilly in the Rhymney Valley; she studied English Literature and Creative Writing at the University of Warwick where she later became a postgraduate fellow, obtaining an MA (Gender and Literature). She is currently a lecturer in English and Creative Writing at the University of Northampton. Her poetry has been widely acclaimed; she won an Eric Gregory Award in 2003 and an Academi Bursary in 2005. Her first collection, *The Secret* was published by Bloodaxe in 2007; as Deryn Rees-Jones noted, this marked the arrival 'of a glittering and ambitious new voice'.

Peter Carpenter is the co-director of Worple Press (www.worplepress.co.uk; authors include two distinguished Welsh poets, Iain Sinclair and John Freeman); he has had four collections of poetry published, most recently *Catch* with Shoestring. He is a regular essayist and reviewer for *Poetry Ireland Review*, *London Magazine* and *Use of English*. He was the University of Reading writer-in-residence for 2007-08 and he has been a Visiting Arts Council Fellow at the University of Warwick since 2000; it was here that he first came across Zoë's work.

*

Peter Carpenter: *When and how did your life as a writer begin? Were there particular contexts that helped to foster your writing?*

Zoë Brigley: My writing life began out of two things: a desire to please and a need to work out problems. It began when I was a child growing up in a single-parent family in South Wales. My mother and I were very close. She had written all her life. She was an organiser, a creative person who used to turn out feminist magazines on a rickety old printer in the 70s and 80s. She wrote two novels that have never been seen by anyone except me. Something held her back – maybe her working class roots and the feeling of uncertainty that gave her. But she has always been indomitable and passed on her love of poetry through performance and the teaching of hundreds of students including me. She wanted me to write and I did. The other side of things is perhaps a sense of loss that came inevitably from my mother and father divorcing and I tend to think that writing poetry in particular became a way of exploring my feelings. Things weren't easy in the 80s, but we came through it together and writing helped.

PC: *You are obviously fascinated by language as a thing in itself and you thank your mother specifically for imbuing a 'love of language'. Two questions. First: Welsh and/ or English?*

ZB: That 'love of language' statement is more political than it might first appear. It is in fact a kind of joke that I was having with my mother and it originates from the film version of Alan Bennett's play, *The History Boys*. There's a scene in the film where Hector, the flamboyant teacher of the 'history boys', describes how he didn't want to create students who would talk about 'the lure of language and their love of words. 'Words' said in that reverential way that is somehow Welsh.' In the film, the line is said with some distaste and I was quite shocked by the offhand prejudice of it. Many of the reviewers quoted this line, but I haven't seen any that challenged it. So many implications here about the Welsh – about their relation to language. The feeling that to describe a 'love of words' is somehow false and pretentious rather than genuine and serious and that this is all somehow bound up with Welsh 'reverence'. When I was thanking people, I knew that my mother would appreciate the gesture of mentioning 'a love of language', a gesture that captures not the idea of being a Welsh windbag, but the pleasure in continuing word-games begun in childhood.

Having said all this, perhaps there is some anxiety for the Welsh in writing in English: having to engage with the immense English poetic tradition, yet seeking something rather different. The English language is always most prominent for me though as my first language. More and more, *Cymraeg* is something that I really only know in snatches and clumps: half-remembered words, lines from poems, refrains from *Cymraeg* hymns and overheard conversation. I think that *Cymraeg* to me has often represented something beyond, something not quite lost but distant, certainly a kind of secret.

PC: *Second: has it remained a matter of 'love' or is it sometimes, as an artist, a love/hate relationship, something more like Eliot's account of the poet's wrangle with words in 'East Coker', every attempt a 'wholly new start', a 'different kind of failure'?*

ZB: I like the word 'failure' and I dislike the word 'perfection'. A friend of mine who writes poetry once told me that he was aiming for perfection in his work. But that idea gives me an odd feeling. It makes me think of Tennyson when he describes the quality of being 'Faultily faultless, icily regular, splendidly null, / Dead perfection, no more.' I was thinking to myself, 'Aren't many wonderful things less than perfect?' Take for example, the armlessness of the Venus de Milo, Marilyn Monroe's mole or the unfinished manuscript of Coleridge's 'Kubla Khan'. I'm not trying for perfection, because, for me, some of the best poetry is flawed, incomplete or broken. Thinking about Eliot too, it's interesting that quite a few people have compared me to him. He certainly was a big influence. I love the incompleteness and fragmented aspect of his poetry and it's in these difficult moments where language is under strain that his poetry is at its best for me.

PC: *In* The Secret *there is a great deal to admire both in the craft and the design of the book. It is incredibly poised and accomplished. How long was it in the making?*

ZB: The book took five years to write. Until recently, I have felt quite annoyed with myself for not working more quickly, because if you join a Creative Writing degree, as I did at Warwick University, you produce so much work as a student, that the normal pace of writing outside an institution seems intolerably slow.

PC: *Would you talk a little about the collection's tri-partite structure?*

ZB: The structure was really important. I like the feeling that each poem has its place and together, there is a kind of accumulation of meaning. The first section to emerge was 'The Lesser Secrets', which includes what I call my 'European' poems that focus particularly on Western culture. Later, 'The Greater Secrets' developed which includes many poems that I wrote when travelling around Mexico and Guatemala. These poems are thinking more about what the West did beyond its own borders and the terrible legacy that remains. The third sequence continues this line of thought, but it has probably been the most controversial. Its title, 'The Curse of the Long-tailed Bird', refers to the Aztec emperor, Montezuma, who according to the Mexicans had a premonition of the Spanish conquest when he was visited by a bird with a mirror in its crest. In the mirror, Montezuma saw troops marching towards Mexico. So there is this mythical story, but the bird came to represent the wealth and riches of Latin America. I was thinking of Eduardo Galeano's book, *The Open Veins of Latin America*, in which he outlines the pillaging of a continent and suggests that the exploitation of Latin America will only stop when the wealth of its natural resources are utterly depleted. The sequence itself melds the Western story of Bluebeard with the history of the Spanish conquest featuring Hernan Cortés as another bearded villain.

PC: *You make full use of the 'myth kitty' at your disposal – a re-working of the story of Blodeuwedd from 'The Mabinogion' (from the cover and opening epigraph onwards) rubbing shoulders with Julia Kristeva and Michel Foucault, for example. This not only fuses the ancient and modern (along the lines of Eliot's mythic method), but also embroils archetypal tropes, figures and narratives with commentators upon cultures and cultural inheritances. Thus you demand a lot of your readers in such dramas of simultaneous considerations. Would you talk a little about your 'method' and also expand a little upon your statement in the notes to the collection that 'as a writer, you are interested in intertextuality'?*

ZB: It's true. Intertextuality is important for me. I definitely see the world through every story that I've ever read. Mythology, folklore and the fairy-tale are particularly important to me, though not necessarily because I want to rewrite the old stories with a new political slant as many writers have done very successfully. What I want to do is take the symbolism of a story and use it to apply to a situation where it is particularly relevant. In *The Secret*, the stories that were important were the Welsh myth of Blodeuwedd, a woman of flowers who plots to murder her husband, and the story of La Malinche, an indigenous Mexican woman who joined Hernan

Cortés' ranks during the Spanish Conquest. There is a sense that the women in the book, who live in a contemporary world, are simply replaying these old stories of supposedly deceitful women who survive nevertheless.

The theorists used are usually telling stories of one kind or another. In *The Secret*, I quote Foucault to complement a narrative about sacrifice and pleasure, while a quotation from Freud is used to frame a poem about sexuality. I also use other sources: Mexican folksongs, a variety of other poets, a medical dictionary, a book on Parkinson's Disease, the Bhagavad-Gita and the Bible. I have always been interested in bringing things together that at first glance seem to be unrelated. It reminds me of Magritte's painting, *The Key to Dreams*, which features what seems to be a child's reading primer, except that the word does not match the picture. An image of a bowler hat is brought together with the word, 'Snow'; a portrait of a candle is subtitled with the word, 'Ceiling'; and so on. I remember seeing that painting and others like it and wondering whether it might be possible to create a poem where disparate objects were brought together. The result was the poem, 'Lonesome City Dweller'.

PC: *David Jones talks in his Preface to* The Anathémata *about the inevitability of an artist showing forth an 'inheritance' in any created work, yet he also makes it clear that such a work is never directly a product of the conscious will: 'Part of my task has been to allow myself to be directed by motifs gathered together from such sources as have by accident been available to me and to make a work out of those mixed data'. How far do you 'allow yourself to be directed' by the 'accident' of sources made available to you?*

ZB: I agree with this in a way. What I would say is that the unconscious sometimes directs us to things that we don't consciously know we are looking for. There is a kind of uncanniness sometimes in finding some motif, some lines or a description that plug in to the very thing that has been preoccupying you. I don't think that it is serendipity. Even when you think that you have found something by accident, you were seeking it all along.

PC: *Does it make a difference to you that readers have even a fleeting acquaintance with your source material? David Jones again: 'If one is making a painting of daffodils what is not instantly involved? Will it make any difference whether or no we have heard of Persephone or Flora or Blodeuedd?'*

ZB: I am in total agreement with Jones. Each of my poems is designed to stand alone. Some people who've read the collection become a bit obsessed with the intertextuality, but that extra layer of complexity that comes with using sources was never my primary concern in writing the poems but only a veneer.

PC: *The use of embroiled allusions makes you a kind of cultural guardian by default. Do you see yourself as such or is there something more playful at work too?*

ZB: I wouldn't cast myself in the role of cultural guardian, more as someone who takes joy in exploring cultures and their stories.

PC: *Many of your poems seem to have affinities to dreams (in sources, an interest in the irrational and the workings of the unconscious, motifs that work across sequences, narrative devices). This creates an artful tension given your powers of formal control. Would you care to talk about this?*

ZB: Dreams have been and are very important for my work. A significant time for me was when I studied psychoanalysis and read Freud's work on dreams and dream language. I read how Lacan described the strategy of dreamwork as being simply another form of metaphor and metonymy. What I try to do in my poems is encode 'reality' through dream language: a series of messages, images, symbols to be decoded. Dreams have inspired the content of poems too, like 'Our Lady of Snows' where a great white arm becomes a frozen river and in the paradoxical triplet of albino twins in 'Ten Fingers, Ten Thumbs'. Interestingly, a careful use of poetic form can lend itself very well to representing the dreams, so in 'Our Lady of Snows', the river/arm metaphor asserts itself again and again in the repetition of a broken villanelle like a recurring dream and 'Ten Fingers, Ten Thumbs' is dominated by a 20 syllable line that represents the disembodied digits. After all, dreams have forms and narratives even if they are unpredictable.

PC: *I thought that one of the collection's major ideas seemed to be some notion of the 'stranger within', ranging from Piaget's 'stranger experience' to Heaney's version of the 'inner émigré'. Thus the otherness of personal experience is often registered via defamiliarisation (political, cultural and linguistic). Does any of this ring true?*

ZB: You are right about the stranger, but the book that most influenced me most was Kristeva's *Strangers to Ourselves*. The book is really about Western culture and how we deal with strangeness or foreignness in others and in ourselves. I like the book because Kristeva rejects the platitude, 'We're all human', which suggests we're all the same. We're *not* all the same and most of the time, we don't even know ourselves. Kristeva says that we can only reach a better understanding by accepting this strangeness and realising that we can't ever know each other fully and totally, just as we don't always understand our own selves and our motives for doing things. Kristeva says, 'If I am a foreigner, there are no foreigners'.

PC: *How did the poems emerge in relation to the sequences we now find them in? Did the concepts for the sequences attract material or did the individual poems develop more organically into the structures?*

ZB: Having a structure is useful for me. Like solving a jigsaw or putting the chess pieces in the right place to find checkmate. Sometimes the poems are dictated by the symbol and its place in the over-arching structure, but at other times poems simply emerge and fit in a more organic way. Having a double impetus to write though can be more generative.

PC: *I have many favourites among the three sequences, poems that stand alone however enmeshed in the contextual forces of the surrounding poems. I have chosen three, one from each section: 'Lonesome City-Dweller', 'The Serpent' and 'The Far Country'. All of them seem to be dealing with forces of violation, threat or isolation and ways of fending these off or accommodating them somehow. Would you like to talk a little about them?*

Lonesome City Dweller

How poor are they that ha' not patience.
What wound did ever heal but by degrees?
　　　　　　　　–William Shakespeare

She is the plain, the eclipse and ruined city
where we walk at dusk through these riverbank tunnels;
that rose in her buttonhole: a tomb for wrestlers.

On the skyline, the dome swells over flatter roofs,
tug-boats on the river and bright windows:
she is the moon and the pavement and stepping shoes.

The riverside cluttered with stalls selling books;
that puppet show features a wooden gentleman
with a bowler hat (from here darkness blooms).

She walks with me in the emptiness of crowds,
while I read that stranger's smile, this woman's frown:
I am the eye and the window and outstretched palm.

Earlier in the café we overheard talk
of her home country, more gossip of strife and death
and she stirred her long drink into a thunderstorm.

Under the bridge she is thinking of her mother:
that crossing in the ruins, that city pocked by gunshot.
She is the dark and desert and memory:
its walls invisible, its boundaries the sky.

ZB: OK, I'll start with 'Lonesome City Dweller'. As I mentioned, it began with an

186

exercise that I set myself to bring into association pairs of symbols that seemed to have nothing in common: a rose and a tomb, a bowler hat and darkness, a cold drink in a glass and a thunderstorm, a closed room and the sky. These symbols were then projected onto a story of a day spent in London with a friend. We were walking along beside the Thames on our way to an event, when she stopped under a bridge and told me how during World War Two, her mother had sheltered from gunfire under just such a bridge. So, yes, the poem is about fending off different kinds of threats and the form (originally a villanelle but now broken) circles around them: the threat that her mother faced, the threat of a memory that returned to my friend and a feeling that somehow it was my fault because of something I said that might have reminded her. Perhaps it is this sense of guilt that made me use Iago's words in Shakespeare's *Othello* for the epigraph, which are meant both ironically and sincerely. The writing of the poem was a way to make up for my mistakes. It was for this reason that I placed the poem tenth in the sequence to represent the Tarot symbol of Temperance. The poem overall admires the self-control of the woman depicted.

Day 5: Serpent

I was angry with my foe
I told it not, my wrath did grow
                    –William Blake

So we spent that first month near an orchard
where the fruit fell down for us to skin;
with teeth, fingers and knives we burrowed in,
we tunnelled in to be hated and tarred.
For women did not know our faces
and tension was keener in villages:
the elders all dead, young men prone to rages
tender and fearful for their birthplaces.
The grudge in them grew till it burst flower
and for us to pick that fig from the tree
was sunlight and cut glass, its trickery
setting the fruit trees ablaze, the tongue sour.
The apple and gun in these hands are mine
and dead is the foe who sees them shine.

'Serpent' is less personal than 'Lonesome City Dweller', because I was trying to work my way into a feeling rather than a personal experience. I was thinking about how most human cultures fear difference and the war in Iraq must have had some influence: the content describes a Western person in a foreign land. The poem is paired with 'Fish-eye' and both are versions of the sonnet, but where as 'Fish-eye' considers the viewpoint of someone being rejected, hurt, spurned, 'Serpent' takes the perspective of the person who acts out the rejection, aggression, hostility. While 'Fish-eye' was a rewriting of the 'Hath not a Jew eyes' speech in Shakespeare's *The Merchant of Venice*, 'Serpent' tries to recreate the feeling of 'The Poison Tree' by William Blake. Blake's poem is a very clever discussion of antagonism and I echo it in the final lines of 'Serpent': 'The apple and gun in these hands are mine / and dead is the foe who sees them shine.' The apple and gun work to suggest a different kind of original sin, where the crime is a lack of tolerance for difference, strangeness, foreignness. Yet this Biblical reading of intolerance is merged with Aztec mythology as the poem is positioned in day five of twenty day round in the Mayan/Aztec calendar. It is a day associated with the serpent, *coatl*, which also recalls the feathered serpent, Quetzalcoatl, for whom Cortés was mistaken on first arriving on his colonizing mission in Central America.

The Far Country

We had to get rid of a Communist government which had taken over.

Under the mountain were four thousand shafts,
now empty: the mossed peak slumps to dead stone,
                    abundant crags decline and topple.
Inside, they sweep out the seams with long brooms.

The blocked temple – its ambit from servitude to dynamo,
                    from powerhouse to slums –
exits flattened: a cathedral springs up in its place,
                    hanging gardens swell in its stead.

Dumb palm trees raise their heads at the prospect of cities;
sunflowers root themselves with cable,
the swift exchange between plant and bulb:
a letter sent to keep the bloodlines joined.

The spade founders, strikes the busy motor
entreating the dead earth. Flags raise their ruddy faces.
Sulphur gives way to frangipani, a loudspeaker opposes
                    her cupped hand.

'The Far Country' is in the same vein as 'Serpent', because I was writing at a time when I had been reading about US government interference in Latin America (again via Eduardo Galeano). It is part of 'The Curse of the Long Tailed Bird', which merges Cortés with Bluebeard and La Malinche with Judith. In writing this version, of the Bluebeard story, I draw on Béla Bartók's opera, *Duke Bluebeard's Castle,* where the heroine has to open not one but seven doors. This door is the fifth and shows La Malinche the far country and the past and present of colonisation and imperialism. The epigraph is an explanation by Dwight D. Eisenhower for interference in the politics of Guatemala, but the admission was only made many years after the violence had happened. The poem was inspired too by a painting: *Self-portrait on the Borderline between Mexico and the United States* by the Mexican artist, Frida Kahlo. The painting shows Kahlo standing between symbols of Mexican and American culture; the sun and moon, a temple and indigenous sculptures represent Mexico, while the US is symbolised by the skyscraper, the factory and the light-bulb. In the earth under Kahlo's feet, the roots of the lush and velvety plants from the Mexican side connect with the wires that run the US's complex technology. This poem tries to explore the exploitation implied in the luscious Mexican plants that feed US industry. The threat in this poem is that of cultural decimation enacted by imperialist cultures and I don't really find a way of solving it, of accommodating it in the poem, because it is still carrying on even today.

PC: *The tale of Blodeuwedd mixes blessing and curse. Do you for example find that your writing practice is radically different when you are writing critical prose or reviews? Does the workaday stuff get in the way – I'm thinking of Ted Hughes, for example, for whom critical prose was a matter of murderous dissection, that he found very destructive in terms of his muse.*

ZB: I do quite a lot of the other kind of writing. I enjoy writing reviews, but I prefer the detail of in-depth critical prose. There is something a little unsatisfying about the cramped space and time of a review. Like trying to pack an elephant in your suitcase as quickly as possible. Writing in more detail can be very satisfying and although aspects of academia can be deadening, there are opportunities to create worthwhile projects. I am co-editing (with Sorcha Gunne) a collection of essays at the moment called *Feminism, Literature and Rape Narratives* to be published by Routledge. This is a project that taps into many of the themes in my poetry: gender, power, resistance, violence and antagonism for example.

PC: *Where do you see yourself in relation to 'Anglo-Welsh' poetic traditions? You seem to go right back to the notion of a Bard in your writing.*

ZB: Sorry to be awkward, but I don't like the term 'Anglo-Welsh'. It's too ambiguous and in the past, it was sometimes used as a stick to beat English language speakers in Wales. You only have to read Ned Thomas' *The Welsh Extremist* to see what I mean.

PC: *I wasn't advocating re-drawing the critical lines with a row of castles on the border. I was thinking more of any affiliations between you and figures such as Edward Thomas thus classified.*

ZB: Fair enough, but thinking about the role of what the Welsh would call a *bardd*, I'm not sure how I feel. If you go back to history of these court poets, their role was to 'sing' to the king about God or the monarchy, to provide heartening battles-songs and to generally entertain. I'm not sure that I'd like to be directed to such a narrow channel. Thinking about Welsh writing in English more generally though, there are many poets that I admire. From the well known poets, I enjoy R.S. Thomas' melancholic self-consciousness, Dylan Thomas for his use of joyful mourning and Gillian Clarke for the sense of oceanic feeling or interconnectedness in her poems. Many of the new Welsh poets are writing as they are now because of these three greats.

PC: *Who have been and are your biggest influences? This might extend to a discussion of the arts in general given the prevalence of visual and musical notation and sources in your writing.*

ZB: In terms of poets, I started as a child with Romantic and Victorian poetry (Coleridge, Keats, Rossetti, Hardy) and then moved on to the Welsh poets I mentioned. As a teenager, I enjoyed Afro-American women poets for their confidence and their rejection of the passive voice and at university, I discovered intensity of metaphor and language (Marina Tsvetaeva, Mina Loy, Rainer Maria Rilke). More recently, I returned to Welsh poetry, having written my PhD thesis on Gwyneth Lewis, Pascale Petit and Deryn Rees-Jones, who are all poets with an interest in overcoming gendered and/or cultural differences.

I can be quite a visual poet and this probably stems from my interest in art and my love of film. In terms of art, I've mentioned Magritte and Kahlo, but film in particular has been such an influence that I wonder whether I should devote some poems to the films that have influenced me most. Flavours of certain films do colour poems from *The Secret*, so that the monotones of Andrew Grieve's *On the Black Hill* and Danny Boyle's *Mr Wroe's Virgins* emerge in 'Blodeuwedd', 'Our Lady of Snows' has icy shades of David Lean's *Doctor Zhivago* and 'Lonesome City Dweller' is bound up with a dizzy intensity and eccentricity that is not unlike the films of Powell and Pressburger, in particular those in colour such as *The Red Shoes* or *Black Narcissus*.

Popular culture in general is a source of inspiration for me, because it has a kind of brutal energy and liveliness. I love detective novels, especially the hard-boiled variety (Chandler, Hammett, McBain and Spillane), for their wit and for the powerful self-assurance of the protagonists. I also enjoy tales of the American West, a favourite of mine being *True Grit* by Charles Portis, in which a young slip of a girl, Mattie Ross, dominates the adults of the book with her indomitable personality. Some Westerns also seem to be about survival and the acceptance of death and loss. Cormac McCarthy's *The Crossing* and the story of a young man's journey with a pregnant wolf was one of the most moving novels that I have ever read. Other types of novels of interest are those that reinvigorate the Arabian myth of Scheherezade and the act of telling a tale every night to survive. Isabel Allende's *House of the*

Spirits is a novel in this vein that has particularly influenced me especially with regard to how Allende deals with the themes of family, violence and gender.

PC: *Where is your work going? Another concept album? Or a series of hit singles? What's next for your readers?*

ZB: It's continuing in the same direction. I'm still trying to work out how to overcome that fear of difference, of the unknown, but more recently I have been working it out more in terms of gender than culture. My current project has been working with the Brontë Parsonage in Haworth to create some poems inspired by belongings of the three Brontë sisters kept in the museum archives. The nineteenth-century is particularly interesting to me as a period of British Empire, of the struggle for the rights of women and the working class. I hope at some point to write some poems using archive material from the wonderful Warwickshire archives, where they have some fascinating documents such as the admittance book for Hatton Asylum and a 'Known Thieves' book from the Birmingham constabulary.

I would also like to write some poems that recycle the symbolism of Hans Christian Andersen's fairy tales. I have been re-reading them recently and the bleak resignation of his stories never fails to move me.

Dannie Abse, Welsh poet and medical doctor, was born in 1923 to Jewish parents. His latest book of poems, *Running Late*, came out in 2006. A recent book, a memoir, *The Presence* (2007), a celebratory portrait of his 50-year marriage, won the Arts Council of Wales Book of the Year award in 2008. He lives, now, in London. His *New Selected Poems 1949-2009* are being published this month by Hutchinson.

Cary Archard edited *Poetry Wales* from 1980 to 1986 and founded the publishing house, Seren Books, in 1981. Among his publications are *Alun Lewis: Collected Poems*, *Alun Lewis: Collected Stories*, *Poetry Wales: 25 Years* and *Welsh Retrospective*. He is also the editor of *Dannie Abse: A Sourcebook*, forthcoming in 2009. His articles have been published in a number of journals and most recently in *Wales at War: Critical Essays on Literature and Art*.

Tiffany Atkinson is a lecturer in English and Creative Writing at Aberystwyth University. She gives regular readings and poetry workshops across England and Wales. She was winner of the Ottakar's and Faber National Poetry Competition (2000) and the Cardiff Academi International Poetry Competition (2001). Her poems are published widely in journals and anthologies, and her first collection, *Kink and Particle* (Seren, 2006) was a Poetry Book Society Recommendation, shortlisted for the Glen Dimplex New Writers' Award, and winner of the Jerwood Aldeburgh First Collection Award (2007).

John Barnie has published nineteen collections of poetry, fiction and essays. *Sea Lilies: Selected Poems 1984-2003* was published by Seren in 2006. His latest book is *Trouble in Heaven* (Gomer 2007).

Idris Caffrey was born in the market town of Rhayader, Mid-Wales. His latest collection is *Relatively Unscathed,* published by Cinnamon Press of North Wales.

Tony Conran was born in India, but has lived mostly in North Wales, where he was a Tutor in English at the University of Bangor. He is well known as a poet, translator and critic with over 20 published books. His translations include *The Penguin Book of Welsh Verse*, 1967 now reissued as *Welsh Verse* (Seren Books); his poetry publications include *Blodeuwedd* (Seren Books 1989), *Castles* (Gomer 1993), and *Red Sap of Love* (Gwasg Carreg Gwalch 2006). His latest volume of poetry *What Brings You Here So Late* has recently been published by Gwasg Carreg Gwalch.

Tony Curtis is Professor of Poetry at the University of Glamorgan where he runs the M.Phil. in Writing. His ninth collection, *Crossing Over*, appeared from Seren in 2007. He continues to write on art in Wales and is also currently working on two books: a selection of the poet, John Tripp, and a personal guide to South Pembrokeshire for the Seren *Real Location* series.

Peter Dale's most recent publications are *Under the Breath*, poems, Anvil, 2002, *Wry-Blue Loves,* a verse translation of Tristan Corbière, Anvil, 2005, a Poetry Book Society Recommendation for Translation, and *Charms* a translation of the poems of Paul Valéry, Anvil, 2007. *Peter Dale in Conversation with Cynthia Haven*, Between the Lines Press, appeared in 2002. His terza rima translation of Dante's *The Divine Comedy*, Anvil, 1996 is now in its sixth edition. A new book of verse, *Local Habitation,* Anvil, is due in spring 2009. He has recently settled in Cardiff.

David Eurig Davies was born in December, 1938 in Pembrokeshire and reared chiefly in Monmouthshire. He spoke Welsh to his grandmother and at Trinity, Cambridge, where he read Natural Sciences for medicine, he discovered a Wales and a literature of which he knew nothing. He ensured his children were exposed to their heritage early. He writes, in English, for fun, and translates some of his daughter's poems, as here.

Damian Walford Davies teaches in the Department of English and Creative Writing at Aberystwyth University. He is the author of *Suit of Lights* (Seren, 2009) and, with Richard Marggraf Turley, of *Whiteout* (Parthian, 2006). He is currently completing a collection entitled *Alabaster Girls*.

William Virgil Davis's forthcoming book is *Landscape and Journey*, winner of the New Criterion Poetry Prize. He has published three other books of poetry: *One Way to Reconstruct the Scene*, which won the Yale Series of Younger Poets Prize; *The Dark Hours*, which won the Calliope Press Chapbook Prize; *Winter Light*. His poems appear regularly in leading journals. He has published in *Poetry, The Nation, The Hudson Review, The Georgia Review, The Gettysburg Review, The New Criterion, The Sewanee Review, The Atlantic Monthly, TriQuarterly, PN Review, Southwest Review*, and in many other journals, including *Agenda*. He has also published half a dozen books of literary criticism, most recently *R. S. Thomas: Poetry and Theology*, as well as scores of critical essays. He is Professor of English and Writer-in-Residence at Baylor University and President of the Texas Institute of Letters.

Stephen Devereux was born in Suffolk and worked in factories and on farms until taking English at UEA in the 1980s. Since then he has taught in schools, colleges and universities in the North West. He has published critical essays and short stories. He began writing poetry for publication in 2005 and has work in many magazines and periodicals, including *Acumen, Envoi, Iota, Poetry Salzburg, The SHOp, Brittle Star, The Interpreter's House, Chimera* and *Other Poetry*. He has worked with the South Bank's Poetry Library and made recordings for their archive.

Menna Elfyn is an award-winning poet and playwright and author of over twenty books, most recently *Peffaith Nam/Perfect Blemish, New & Selected Poems 1995-2007* (Bloodaxe, 2007); her work has been translated into 18 languages. A fortnightly columnist for the *Western* Mail since 1995 , she is also Royal Literary Fellow at Swansea University and Writing Director of the Masters programme in Creative Writing at Trinity University College. In 2008, she won a Creative Arts award to write a book on the subject of 'Sleep'. In 2002, she was made 'Bardd Plant', Poet Laureate for the Children of Wales.

Christine Evans: Born in west Yorkshire, she came to Llŷn as a teacher of English more than forty years ago. *Selected Poems* (Seren) won the inaugural Roland Mathias Prize in 2005 with praise for a 'fresh eye and boldness of metaphor, a sense of living on the threshold of other worlds.' *Burning the Candle* has been called 'a major contribution to Anglo-Welsh poetry' and *Growth Rings* was shortlisted for Welsh Book of the Year in 2007. Her latest work is *Bardsey* (Gomer, 2008), a collection of essays, poems and photographs.

Peter Finch was born in Cardiff where he still lives. For twenty years he ran the Oriel Bookshop and is now Chief Executive of Academi, the Literature Promotion Agency for Wales. His prose books include *Real Cardiff* and *Real Wales*. His *Selected Poems* has just been published by Seren.

Ian Gregson's latest book of poems is *How We Met* (Salt, 2008). *Call Centre Love Song*, a selection of his poems, was shortlisted for the prestigious Forward Prize. His poems and reviews have appeared in the *London Review of Books*, the *TLS* and *Poetry Review*, amongst others. His critical books are: *Contemporary Poetry and Postmodernism, The Male Image: Representations of Masculinity in Postwar Poetry* (both published by McMillan), *Postmodern Literature* (Hodder Arnold, 2004) and *The New Poetry in Wales* (University of Wales Press, 2007). Since 1977 he has taught in the English department at the university in Bangor and he is now a Professor there.

Marc Harris was born in Cardiff in 1962. He spent thirty years living in England and returned to Cardiff to live in the year 2000. His poems have been published widely in journals and magazines in Wales, the U.K., New Zealand and the U.S. He has read his poetry at the Wales Milennium Centre and his poems have been exhibited with paintings at an exhibition in Saint David's Hall in the Welsh capital. He works with homeless people in Cardiff and is a volunteer for the RSPB.

Wendy Holborow is a Welsh woman living and working in Corfu, though she spends several months a year in Swansea with her daughter. She has won several prizes for short stories and poetry, a lot of which have been published in the UK and internationally. Founder and co-editor of *Poetry Greece* for several years, she now writes a regular page on Greek poetry for an Anglo-Greek magazine. She is working on her first collection of poetry as well as a time-slip novel set in the present time and 19th Century Greece.

Mererid Hopwood comes from Cardiff though her family roots are in Pembrokeshire. She now lives in Carmarthen with her family. She was awarded a first class honours in Spanish and German from Aberystwyth and a PhD from University College, London. She teaches full-time, sharing the week between the School of Languages at the University in Swansea and the Welsh-medium comprehensive, Ysgol Gyfun Gymraeg Bro Myrddin. She has won the Chair and Crown for poetry at the National Eisteddfod and the Prose Medal for her first novel.

Nigel Jenkins was born on a farm in Gower and worked as a newspaper reporter in the English Midlands before returning home to work as a freelance writer and lecturer. His latest book of poems is *O For a Gun* (Planet Books, 2007). His book about Welsh missionaries in north-east India, *Gwalia in Khasia* (Gomer, 1995), won the Wales Book of the Year award in 1996. His selected essays and articles, *Footsore on the Frontier* (Gomer Press), was published in 2001. Co-editor of *The Welsh Academy Encyclopaedia of Wales* (2008), he published in 2008 *Real Swansea*, a work of psychogeography about his home town. He teaches creative writing at Swansea University.

Roland John has had a long association with *Agenda*. His prose books include *A Beginner's Guide to The Cantos of Ezra Pound*. His latest poetry collection is *A Lament for England* (bluechrome). He is the only member of his immediate family that is not Welsh speaking.

Dylan Jones has published one full-length collection of poetry, *Dreaming Nightly of Dragons* (University of Salzburg 1996). He has also contributed to a number of poetry anthologies including *The Poet's House* (Gomer 2000), *The Lie of the Land* (Cinnamon Press 2006) and *Only Connect* (Cinnamon Press 2007). He is a gardener, a self-taught artist, and a singer with the folk/roots collective, The Sheiling.

Chris Kinsey was BBC Wildlife Poet of the Year in 2008. She received an Arts Council of Wales Writer's Bursary in 2000. Her collection, *Kung Fu Lullabies*, Ragged Raven Press, came out in 2004; her second, *Swarf,* is forthcoming from Smokestack Books. Chris has read at various Poetry Cafés across the UK, at Ledbury Festival and as part of the Poets for Oxfam readings in London. She is on the board of Ty Newydd, The National Writing Centre for Wales

Gwyneth Lewis was the first National Poet of Wales from 2005-06. *Chaotic Angels* collects her first three books of poetry in English and *Tair Mewn Un* (*Three in One*) her books in Welsh, her first language. She also writes non-fiction: *Sunbathing in the Rain: A Cheerful Book on Depression* and *Two in a Boat: A Marital Voyage*. She is an award-winning playwright and has written three libretti for Welsh National Opera. She is currently living in the US.

Yang Lian, the Chinese poet, was born in 1955 in Bern, Switzerland where his diplomat parents were stationed. He grew up in Beijing during the cultural revolution. As an exile, he lived for many years in Auckland, New Zealand, and he has been based in London since 1994. His poetry has been translated into more than twenty languages.

Johnny Marsh is an art psychotherapist and artist living and working in Sussex.

Andrew McNeillie, for the past five years Literature Editor at OUP, has recently been appointed to a professorial chair at Exeter University. This is in connection with his magazine *Archipelago* which is to provide the focal point for a new MA: 'Nature, Writing and Place', to run from September 2009 at Exeter's Cornwall campus. He has a memoir *Once* forthcoming from Seren in May 2009. A book of poems *In Mortal Memory* is due from Carcanet in February 2010. His books include *Nevermore* (2000), *Now, Then* (2002), *Slower* (2006), and the prose memoir *An Aran Keening* (2001).

Kathy Miles was born and brought up in Liverpool. She moved to Wales in 1972 to study English Literature at the University of Wales Lampeter, and now works there as an Assistant Librarian in the University Library. She has published two books: *The Rocking-Stone* (Poetry Wales Press) and *The Third Day: Landscape and the Word* (Gomer) and her poetry frequently appears in magazines and anthologies, including the 2008 Forward Book of Poetry. A collection of her work, *The Shadow-House*, is due to be published by Cinnamon Press in November 2009.

Sam Milne is a Scottish poet living in Surrey. His books of poems include *Twa-Three Lines* and *Sangs o Luve and Pairtan*. He has published a critical monograph on the poetry of Geoffrey Hill. He is currently writing essays on Imagism, Flora Garry and Laura (Riding) Jackson.

Robert Minhinnick's *King Driftwood* appeared from Carcanet in 2008. His novel, *Sea Holly* (Seren), was shortlisted for the 2008 RSL Ondaatje Prize. Between 1997 and 2008 he edited *Poetry Wales*. He has twice won the Forward Prize for the 'best individual poem'. He lives in Porthcawl, where he is an advisor to the charity, 'Sustainable Wales'.

Steven O'Brien's mother came from Ferndale in the Rhonnda. His father, a great traditional singer, comes from Monasterevin in Co.Kildare, Ireland. He attributes the Welsh/Irish crucible of his childhood – full of religious passion and political fire, lit by songs and the relish of words – to making him what he is today as a poet. He lectures in Creative Writing at the University of Portsmouth and lives in Worthing. His first collection, *Dark Hill Dreams*, was brought out by *Agenda* Editions.

Pascale Petit's latest collection is *The Treekeeper's Tale* (Seren, 2008) and a fifth, *What the Water Gave Me - Poems after Frida Kahlo*, is due from Seren in 2010. Her previous collections, *The Huntress* and *The Zoo Father* (Seren), were both shortlisted for the T S Eliot Prize and were books of the year in the *TLS*. In 2007-8 she took part in the Yellow Mountain Poetry Festival in China and the UK. She tutors creative writing at Tate Modern and is the Royal Literary Fund Fellow at Middlesex University.

Sheenagh Pugh lives in Cardiff, though possibly not for much longer. She has published many collections with Seren, the latest being *Long-Haul Travellers* (2008), which has been shortlisted for the Roland Mathias Prize. Her previous collection, *The Movement of Bodies,* was shortlisted for the T S Eliot Prize. She has also published two novels and a critical study on fan fiction, *The Democratic Genre* (Seren 2005).

Lynn Roberts has had poems published in *Outposts* and *Lighten Up Online*; she has won prizes in The Writers' Bureau (2006) and Envoi International (2008) competitions, and had poems shortlisted for many poetry prizes. She has just won the Listowel Writers' Week Poetry Collection competition. She specialises in the history of picture frames and is co-author of *A History of European Picture Frames* and *Frameworks* (both 1996). As a researcher and archivist, she works for Paul Mitchell, and also for the National Portrait Gallery on the picture frame section of the NPG website. She is also an artist. Her father's family comes from Rhyll.

Paul Robichaud is an assistant Professor of English at Albertus Magnus College in New Haven, Connecticut. His poems have appeared in *The Hudson Review* (2005) and *Palimpsest: Yale Literary and Arts Magazine* (2003). His most recent publication is a critical study of the poetry of David Jones, *Making the Past Present* (Catholic University of America Press, 2007). He has travelled throughout Wales and launched his book at the National Library in 2007. A native of Toronto, Canada, he and his wife have lived in America for eight years.

Zoë Skoulding's most recent collection of poems, *Remains of a Future City*, was published by Seren in 2008, following *The Mirror Trade* in 2004. *Dark Wires*, a collaboration with Ian Davidson, was published by West House Books in 2007. She holds an AHRC Fellowship in the Creative and Performing Arts at Bangor University, where she is researching poetry and city space. She is a co-editor of *Skald* and became editor of *Poetry Wales* in 2008.

Edward Storey was born in Cambridgeshire where his early work (poetry and prose) was influenced by the Fens. At the same time he lived for many years with a Welsh family from the Rhondda and made regular visits with them to the Valleys. Poems then began to appear in *The Anglo-Welsh Review* and *Poetry Wales*. In 1999 he and his wife (who grew up on Anglesey) moved to Wales and now live at Discoed, near Offa's Dyke. He has published ten volumes of poetry, several volumes of prose, and written for radio and television.

Richard Marggraf Turley lectures in English Literature and Creative Writing at the University of Wales, Aberystwyth. His poems have appeared in *Poetry and Audience, Planet* and *Agenda*, as well as elsewhere. His co-authored first collection, *Whiteout*, came out from Parthian Books in 2007.

Gerry Wells lives in Rutland. His poetry and short stories have appeared in many periodicals and various BBC programmes. He has published five collections of poetry and has had work selected for a number of anthologies. He has been a soldier, farmer and lecturer and is now happily retired with time enough to write.

Jeni Williams teaches literature and art history at Trinity University College, Carmarthen. She has published widely in magazines including *New Welsh Review, New Writing, The London Magazine, Poetry Wales, Orbis* and *Planet*. She has contributed to collections of Welsh/refugee writing and was contributing editor of *Fragments from the Dark: Women Writing Home and Self in Wales* (2008), an anthology of Welsh women's writing together with poetry, testimonies and stories by asylum seeking and refugee women. Her first collection, *Being the Famous Ones*, is published by Parthian this autumn.

Philip Williams was born in South Wales in 1961. He emigrated to Australia with his parents and twin brother in the early '60s, returning in 1966. He owes his interest in poetry to inspirational teachers at Llantarnam Comprehensive School and visits by notable Anglo-Welsh poets such as Dannie Abse, John Idris Jones and Gillian Clarke. A graduate of Leeds University he has worked in PR and marketing and is now Head of Marketing at Keele University. He is married with two daughters.

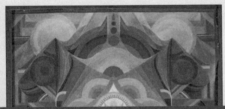

AGENDA editions

STEVEN O'BRIEN

DARK HILL DREAMS

AGENDA EDITIONS

When I read Steven O'Brien's poems I get this feeling of a voice that includes bardic splendour, ballad vigour, the professional storyteller's magnetism, and the presence of a deep humanism that never fails to celebrate the music and the mystery of life. O'Brien travels through the centuries and cultures, and emerges with his own lucid, complex voice.   Brendan Kennelly

ISBN 0-902400-79-7   Price £10.00 incl p&p UK

Another Welsh poet published by Agenda Editions:
Keith Jones: Merrimans £7.99

Seren: a leading publisher of poetry, based in Wales

Collections by Paul Henry, Tony Curtis, Ruth Bidgood, Zoë Skoulding, Sheenagh Pugh and Meirion Jordan are reviewed in this issue of *Agenda*.

But quality rather than geography is the prerequisite for publication. *Letter to Patience* by John Haynes won the Costa Poetry Award 2006. Kathryn Simmonds' *Sunday at the Skin Launderette* was shortlisted for the Costa Award 2008 and the Glen Dimplex First Book Award, and won the Forward Prize for Best First Collection.

Tiffany Atkinson won the Jerwood Aldeburgh Prize for *Kink and Particle*. Sheenagh Pugh's *Long-Haul Travellers* is longlisted for this year's Wales Book of the Year. Her *Later Selected Poems* appears in June.

"I can't call a more exciting début to mind" wrote Sarah Crown of Meirion Jordan's *Moonrise*. At the opposite end of the spectrum, age-wise, is *Time Being*, Ruth Bidgood's tenth collection in five decades of writing, which is a PBS Recommendation. Carol Rumens' *Blind Spots*, is "her best work ever" according to the *Independent*.

The landmark anthology *Women's Work* is one of the top ten poetry books selected by Poetry Society Director Judith Palmer in the *Independent*. Edited by Seren's long-time poetry editor Amy Wack and American poet and critic Eva Salzman, it runs to 364 pages and features poetry from across the English-speaking world.

All this, plus the influential quarterly magazine *Poetry Wales*, now edited by Zoë Skoulding, with a distinct international agenda.

www.seren-books.com

57 Nolton Street, Bridgend CF31 3AE 01656 663018

TEAR–OFF SUBSCRIPTION FORM

Pay by cheque (payable to 'Agenda'), or
Visa / MasterCard

SUBSCRIPTION RATES ON INSIDE FRONT COVER

1 Subscription (1 year) =

2 double issues 1 double, 2 single issues or 4 single issues (The above is variable)

Please print

Name: ....

Address: ....

....

....

.... Postcode..

Tel: ....

Email: ....

Visa / MasterCard No: □□□ – □□□ – □□□ – □□

Expiry date: □□ – □□

Please tick box:

New Subscription □   Renewed Subscription □

(or subscribe online – www.agendapoetry.co.uk)

Send to: AGENDA, The Wheelwrights, Fletching Street, Mayfield,
East Sussex, TN20 6TL